5/10/19
To my dear Aunt Pucky ~
you've been such a caring
supporter of my writing...
Love, Mag

BOWING TO

ELEPHANTS

Tales *of a* Travel Junkie

Th D0169660 *s P 75*

Veronica Landy

MAG DIMOND

SHE WRITES PRESS

Published September 2019
Printed in the United States of America
Print ISBN: 978-1-63152-596-4
E-ISBN: 978-1-63152-597-1
Library of Congress Control Number: 2019937405

For information, address:
She Writes Press
1569 Solano Ave #546
Berkeley, CA 94707

Interior design by Tabitha Lahr

She Writes Press is a division of SparkPoint Studio, LLC.

Names and identifying characteristics have been changed to protect the privacy of certain individuals.

Mag's telephone numbers since
2/11/19
SF 415 359 9757
cell 415 423 7742
24 White street address
zip 94109

BOWING TO

ELEPHANTS

Book arrived

24 White Street
SF 94109
Granduecth
Havinia
Dimonds
San Francisco 1953

MY NYC TAXI

Buehism

P 113 _ Doug

To Lavinia Dimond, my grandmother, my hero, who shaped my path.

To Madeleine Violett, my reckless mother, who offered beauty and broke my heart.

CONTENTS

Introduction | 11

One: The Beginning of My Traveling Life—Florence | 13

Two: Beauty and Pleasure in Paris | 29

Three: Alone in Venice in January | 51

Four: Burma Pilgrimage | 71

Five: Spiritual Practice in Bhutan | 103

Six: Duality and Impermanence in India | 125

Seven: Falling in Love with Elephants in Kenya | 147

Eight: On Not Knowing Vietnam | 165

Nine: Shadow of Death in Cambodia | 191

Ten: Coming Home to San Francisco | 209

Acknowledgments | 251

About the Author | 253

"In these memoirs or recollections there are gaps here and there, and sometimes they are also forgetful, because life is like that. . . . Many of the things I remember have blurred as I recalled them, they have crumbled to dust, like irreparably shattered glass."

—Pablo Neruda, *Memoirs*

"In probing my childhood (which is the next best thing to probing one's eternity), I see the awakening of consciousness as a series of spaced flashes, with the intervals between them gradually diminishing until bright blocks of perception are formed, affording memory a slippery hold."

—Vladimir Nabokov, *Speak Memory*

Introduction

The journey of exploring one's past is circuitous, and often painful and complicated. One has to peel away layer after layer of fragile and ephemeral memory to find the story. I discovered in my search that I needed to move backward and forward in time in order to find the "through line" of my narrative.

I began this book as a series of essays about my travels to far-flung places, and what I discovered as I wrote the pieces was that certain characters from my past life showed up and asked to be heard; they reminded me of cultural and intellectual gifts, some loving kindness, and frequent interludes of profound neglect and loneliness threaded through my childhood. It appeared that this memoir was not just about being a world traveler, but it was also about the early internal yearnings that propelled me to specific places. In the end, it was the story of discovering my authentic self and learning how to love by exploring foreign lands.

It all begins as I ask my mother an urgent question that demands witnessing and truth, and the honest answer I'm seeking does not come. My family was falling apart, and the woman whose love I desperately sought couldn't admit it or comfort me. From this time forward, my young life would become a journey *to understand the truth* of things. The chapters in this memoir illustrate how most of my adult adventures have been, in a way, responses to earlier questions lurking in my heart and mind from the time I was a girl (Why do people separate themselves by class? How is it that art and music nourish the human spirit? What are we to make of death? How do we find love?). In each chapter I've woven together my present-day travel stories with those emotional scenarios from my childhood and adolescence that had pushed me to become a traveler.

I wish you a thought-provoking adventure as you traverse the mosaic of my present and past lives. You won't get lost, I promise, and you may at times find that the winding trajectory offers unexpected and moving sensory experiences that *invite you in* . . . to smile and reflect, and to be reminded of the many rich stories your own heart is holding.

One: The Beginning of
My Traveling Life—Florence

I had been waiting so long to ask her my question.
Waiting as she moved from her bed to the dresser to put away her underthings, waiting as she stopped to light a cigarette, waiting as she stared at her huge pink-and-red painting on the bedroom wall. I sat cross-legged on her bed in the late afternoon, staring at the floor and trying my best to be patient. I was pretty good at that for an eight-year-old. . . . But I was tired, a little scared, and confused.

There had been a much longer waiting before. Several years at least of watching my mother and father slowly fall away from each other and from me, sitting over creamed spinach at the dinner table, cocktails in the living room, or driving silently in the car. I saw it all: the meanness and the fear. You see, from the beginning I was a witness.

A couple of nights before this, I had lain in my bed in the dark and heard her scream at him, and then there was silence. Some nights before that, I had heard a telephone being hurled at the wall as she shrieked, "You never listen to me—I don't. . . ." (And then I couldn't hear the rest.)

"It's all impossible!" I felt invisible in my dark room with the nightlight burned out, and pretty soon a cold wiggly fear came. I tried to hear what was happening in the living room—I needed to know what it was, or at least I thought I did, but what I really wanted was to burrow deeper under my blankets to sleep and forget.

I fixed my eyes on her now as she continued to busy herself with her laundry, and then I finally spit it out. "Mom, I have something to ask you."

Instead of answering me, she asked, "Oh, by the way, Maggie, did you remember to feed the cat?"

"Well, of course I did! I always do." My voice began to sound louder and a bit braver.

"Yes, now just what *is* this question of yours?"

Her mind was on something else then, I could tell, and for a fraction of a moment I just stared at her movie star looks in the early evening sunlight, that beauty that set her apart that I knew would never be mine. She looked at me now, as though daring me to speak.

"Mom—are you and Daddy *okay*? Are we going to be all right? I'm worried—"

"Of course, we're all right!" she replied too quickly. "What made you think that? Everything is fine. You fret too much, my dear." She was trying to reassure, I could see it, but her tone was too chilly.

"But I heard you both yelling. Just the other night . . . and some nights before that. . . ." I wanted her to hug me or just touch my face with her fingertips, but instead she reached over to the dresser for her comb, ran it through her straight brown hair, and pursed her red lips in the mirror.

"Nothing is the matter. You must learn to not be so horribly serious all the time."

Less than a month later, I sat on my grandmother's large

gray sofa in her living room as she cautiously announced to me that my parents were going to divorce, that my father would be going away. I remember thinking she was telling me so my mother didn't have to. She was doing it *for* her daughter-in-law, who had a hard time being honest with her family. Her hazel eyes were soft and moist and filled with affection as she looked right at me, ready to offer comfort.

"That's all right, Grandmother. Now the fighting will stop, I guess," I said with a big sigh. I didn't have anything else to say; I think I felt relief that soon I'd escape the war zone I'd been living in. I was just as calm as my grandmother, and quite collected for an eight-year-old.

Frozen in that moment of composure and skewed logic, I knew my mother had not told me the truth, and I wanted to believe it was because she just didn't know how. Nobody ever taught her to. . . . Was this all happening because she just didn't see me, or because speaking the truth was too frightening? Or both? In the end it didn't really matter, for soon I would simply become the invisible child she was stuck with, the little girl who sat quietly through long dinners waiting for her chance to speak and be heard, trying to decipher the people around her so she could learn how to fit in. From here on, my mother and I would be uncomfortably bound to one another. I was an unavoidable player in her life, and my path as witness of my life and carrier of fragile memory was set.

I remember months of brooding silently in our little Belvedere house on the lagoon, waiting for something to happen. And then my father packed up his gray suits and brown loafers and left quietly and without ceremony, as was his nature. Before too long, I was watching my mother and some of her artist friends having a moving party, wrapping pots and pans in plain paper and taping up boxes and occasionally raising their wine glasses in a triumphant gesture.

I was in charge only of packing up my clothes and stuffed animals and making sure that I didn't forget any of my books. When I wasn't rummaging in my room trying to be useful, I sat at the kitchen table and just watched her. She caught me staring at her, tossing her hair aside with a quick move. "Maggie,"—she always called me "Maggie" when she was not in a loving mood—"how many times do I have to tell you not to stare like that? Sulking is very unattractive, you know. It didn't work out with your father because I just didn't love him anymore. . . . That's all there is to it! You'll get over it." And with that, she returned to her boxes, her wine, and her friends.

Some months later, we traveled across the Golden Gate Bridge to live together in a Victorian apartment in San Francisco, just my restless mother, myself, and Rhubarb the Siamese cat. My traveling life had begun.

I hold an old memory now. From the haze of many years it comes into focus: the Tuscan hills lit up in autumn in burnished golds and reds, softening my heart. As evening descended on the city of Florence and the cypresses stood tall and proud around the old stone house on this fall day, our little family began to settle in for an evening in the villa. My mother had packed us up, my stepfather and me, and led us off to Italy so she could be close to art—as far as I knew, that was the reason. She had spent several years in art school in the early fifties, after we moved to San Francisco from the East, and had adopted the bohemian artist's path when she was married to my father. She appeared to be driven by beauty, its creation and acquisition. She had been so stunning as a young woman and so conditioned to being called beautiful that she became obsessed with the *idea* of the beautiful life as she grew older—perhaps. Or maybe she saw her future as some sort of blank canvas waiting for the right eyes. This dream, along with her own trust fund income, brought us to the Villa dei Cipressi above Florence in 1956. There had been other moves before this one, in between the uneventful divorce from my father and a quick marriage to a man she had met while working as a cocktail waitress at the Tin Angel, a San Francisco jazz club. My stepfather, Raymond, was smart and eccentric, raised with many siblings in a poor Norwegian immigrant family from Brooklyn. He loved books and drawing and had a handsome angular face scarred by childhood smallpox. I was becoming used to moving by this time, and just put my head down and forged ahead the way I had to when she failed to explain the reasons for her choices. I don't remember being either scared or excited about moving to a foreign country thousands of miles away when I was only eleven.

That evening in Florence, the sun had finally gone down, and we sat around our large oval dining table as candles cast a small umbrella of light above us in the giant stone *sala*. Steaming pasta with butter, a big bowl of Parmesan, a roast of pork all perfumed with rosemary and surrounded by shiny dark green zucchini and brilliant tomatoes, and of course, a salad of beautiful wild lettuces. My mother had put the red wine in a glass carafe where it shone like a ruby. She always knew how to create a beautiful picture. We even had soft white cloth napkins and white plates with little gold edges on them.

As she and Raymond served up the food, they talked about how they had to find a cook and housemaid to cope with our needs, while I wondered about the unusual little school I was going to and the possibility of finding new friends there. They clinked glasses ceremoniously, and she exclaimed with a broad smile, "Isn't it too divine, Mag? Here we are in the most beautiful country ever! Aren't you happy, darling?" I wasn't sure about the "divine" part. I hadn't fallen for this place yet—it had all happened so fast, after all, the divorce and the new husband—I just wasn't ready to be charmed. But I was just a little curious about starting seventh grade with a bunch of American expats in an ancient Italian palazzo. She didn't wait for my answer to her question about being happy but turned toward my new stepfather to issue instructions about the necessary calls in the morning so we could get some domestic help.

So off I went to Miss Barrie's American School, housed in a huge dark, damp-smelling building on the Via dei Bardi on the right side of the Arno across from the city center. A tiny dowager, a certain Miss Barrie from Boston ran the place quite invisibly, relegating the mechanics to Mr. Faust, an imposing tall gentleman who sported large, horn-rimmed eyeglasses and Old-World manners. There were about twenty-four of us in all at the school, a motley crew of young Americans aged about eleven to sixteen, thrown together in Latin, Italian, and English classes, and huddling on cold mornings while Mr. Faust intoned the basics of algebra to us in his German accent. Looking back, I mostly remember the dark main room with the large oval table and a rickety ancient iron chandelier hanging down from above, where our little voices echoed dramatically against the high ceiling, and how the room was lit up periodically by the perky Miss Barrie herself, looking the part of Bostonian matron in her crisp dark suit and ruffled white blouse, as she announced in perfect diction, "Now, boys and girls, we are going to go on a grand journey to discover the beautiful mind of William Shakespeare. . . ." I believed in her from the very beginning.

Our school was a claustrophobic little world, really, but I felt comforted by the closeness; it made getting used to all things foreign easier. Eventually I found a young boy with pearly white complexion and pale blond hair to focus my attention on, and I spent many hours trying to make myself known to him. I must have succeeded, because before long Michael and I were writing little personal notes to one another, delivering them into jacket pockets in the coat closet, or passing them off directly in class under the large table when we happened to be sitting next to one another. Living with this little secret was exciting and strangely familiar, like the times I used to hide chocolate candy bars for myself in my desk back home, or rifle through my mother's dresser drawer to smell the lavender sachet and feel the soft things she put there. I understood concealment. This boy and I knew something different was up between us as we grinned stupidly at each other across the rooms we inhabited at Miss Barrie's, but I'm not sure we knew to call it love.

Back at the villa later in the afternoon, I sat in my bedroom with high ceilings and wrote in my red leather journal about feeling lonely and confused by my beautiful mother, who preferred her evening cocktails to my company. I was alien to her, as her company had been probably been alien to her mother long before. Even though she had been tended in childhood by governesses and such, my mother chose a new and modern look to her life, without any nannies, of course, and I was simply overlooked. I wrote too about Michael and me, and about how adorable my stepfather, Raymond, was. I think I had a crush on him from the start, which he seemed to encourage—he often smiled right at me and made plenty of time to talk; he appeared to like me a lot. Some nights he sat with me in my bedroom and sang the same mournful English ballad, "Greensleeves," again and again in his strange atonal voice, making me feel quite special.

Before long we had the warm bountiful company of our new cook, Elda, in the house, and she served us our dinner in the giant living room by candlelight, of course: a big white tureen of soup and platters of steaming eggy fettuccini, crusty *scaloppine alla Milanese*, and a perfect green salad. *"Ecco, il pranzo! Buon appetito!"* she'd announce proudly as she beamed at my mother and the rest of us. She soon became my hero, and I followed her, many afternoons after school, into the kitchen and stayed to watch her do her magic there. She made creamy mayonnaise from scratch, pouring the thick olive oil into the egg with reverence, and *straciatella* soup—golden chicken broth with whipped eggs in it—as well as a spaghetti *carbonara*, hearty peasant pasta with salt pork and egg, lots of butter and cheese.

I often gave up my journal writing to sit with her in the kitchen as warm light poured through the windows from the west, and I watched her gently wash dark leaves of basil, slice perfect tomatoes, and grate parmesan while humming a warm melody to herself. When she picked up a chicken to prepare, she did it with joy, patting its plump pink body with her big hands that were dark red from all her hard work, smearing the olive oil all over, and stuffing it with big handfuls of rosemary. She had handpicked that very chicken from the butcher's that morning and knew it to be the perfect one for our dinner. Every once in a while, I accompanied her on her shopping trips and watched as she joined the animated conversation with the cheese man, the produce lady, or the baker with his huge white floury arms, both of Elda's hands moving continuously to persuade and cajole, everyone's voices rising and falling. It was opera and dance right there in the morning sunshine. I learned in those moments just how seriously Italians took the daily gathering of food.

My mother had been a pretty good cook when I was younger, but this buxom young woman who tended our kitchen was a magician. She had huge breasts and dark hair that fell down her back in giant waves, and eyes that flashed dark and loving. She taught me the vocabulary and the dance of food. The lettuces were *belissime* (most beautiful), the tomatoes *meravigliosi* (marvelous), the chicken *perfetta-mente fresco* (perfectly fresh). She took a purple eggplant and sliced it into perfect white disks, she held a shiny red pepper in her hands as though it were sacred, cutting it then into perfect rings on the wooden board, and she examined all the different lettuces and wild greens with great care before tossing them in the salad bowl. She saw me observing her. She lit up the kitchen with animated gratitude, a deep husky laugh coming from her expansive body as she began to share stories of growing up in southern Italy. *"Vuoi sentire una storia della mia vita in Calabria?"* You want to hear a story of life in Calabria? I was studying Italian at Miss Barrie's then, but it was from Elda that I really got the language. *And the food, of course.* She and I ate and talked together as days and months passed; we laughed, chopped vegetables, poured golden olive oil, whipped eggs, grated mountains of cheese, and found friendship.

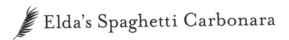 Elda's Spaghetti Carbonara

> *4 eggs beaten*
> *1 pound bacon, cut into small squares*
> *½ stick unsalted butter, cut into bits*
> *¾–1 cup coarsely grated Parmesan*
> *Salt and fresh ground pepper to taste*
> *1 pound spaghetti*

> Cook bacon in a skillet (we used a crude salt pork when in Italy), draining off fat.

Cook pasta in large (8 quart) pot of salted boiling water until al dente, firm but not hard. Drain.

Toss steaming pasta in large bowl with beaten eggs (thus cooking the eggs), cooked bacon, butter, and grated Parmesan. Add salt and pepper to taste. Serve with extra parmesan on the side (you can never have too much cheese!).

Serves 4.

The year in Florence was a tender year when I found what felt like love, as my mother and Raymond joined Florence's claustrophobic expatriate society. On Saturdays, Michael and I took off for the movies where we sat in the dark and held hands while watching one of Elvis Presley's latest hits, like *Love Me Tender.* By the end of the fifties, Elvis movies had made a huge splash in Italy, and what made the experience so surreal was that they were always dubbed in Italian except for the singing. Elvis's deep sexy voice touched me inside and made me believe in romance, as I leaned in closer to Michael in the dark theater and inhaled his tweed jacket.

During the week, Raymond usually helped me with my readings and essays; I eventually understood that tending to my academic tasks had been one of the reasons my mother married him. He treated me as though I were a grownup, which amused and bothered me at the same time, because it really wasn't true. He took his new parenting role seriously but wasn't very good at expressing his feelings, a trait he shared with my mother. Every once in a while, she actually saw me, and she'd stare at me through the cigarette smoke and proclaime proudly that I was the "perfect" child, particularly when she was surrounded by her friends. I was "perfect" then,

I suspect, because I was quiet and compliant, and because I now looked elsewhere for love. Later, when I was in my forties and feeling unusually vulnerable, she once gave me, for no reason, a little needlepoint pillow that announced "my daughter is perfect" in white against a pink background, and I was speechless with the irony of it all. I think we both were. There had been nothing perfect about our relationship. We lived together through many years in separate bubbles, with rare, usually unsuccessful, attempts on my part to be seen and cherished, and occasional extravagant gifts from her to dazzle me . . . which made us an awkward pair indeed.

I was eleven that year in Florence, on the verge of falling into love and romance, which I was reminded of everywhere I went: the Elvis Presley movies, Italian love songs pouring out of apartment windows, Shakespearean sonnets delivered by Miss Barrie, Elda's love affair with food in the kitchen, and lurking in the ancient stones and alleyways, the story we had been told in Italian class of Dante and his Beatrice. We were being taught rudimentary Dante then, and beginning to explore his *Inferno* and listen to the sad tale of his romance with the noble and distant Beatrice. I found myself visualizing Michael and me disappearing into their story as we walked up the damp *lungarno* toward the Ponte Vecchio. Following the failure of his love affair, Dante made this woman the muse for his entire body of written work, which kept her in his mind and heart for his entire life.

Dante's *Inferno* later became one of my most deeply loved works in literature. As I continued studying the poet and his words over the years, I learned that a brilliant mind was no defense against loneliness and exile. As part of the White Guelph "family," Dante eventually found himself on the wrong side of a bitter civil war in the city and was banished from his beloved Florence at the age of thirty-six.

I have lived in the world of literature for as long as I can remember, and have always been drawn to exiles, whether it was Homer's Odysseus trying to find his way home, Pablo Neruda whose conscience drove him from his homeland, or the wild Irishman James Joyce who only fulfilled his vision when living outside his own country. I noticed that comfort and acceptance eventually came to those who were far away, but it was usually an ease tempered with grief, long sad years of drinking to forget and writing in order to remember. I began to know this as I grew up a shadow in my mother's company, trying to discover my own authentic story.

Reading the *Inferno* marked the beginning of my ongoing curiosity about the hero's journey, the passage all humans take as they move forward while holding in their hearts what came before. I wanted to see my life and the lives of others in the context of epic storytelling and grasp the interconnection of all human endeavors. In Hell, Dante reflects on many painful human qualities—misguided love, corruption, deceit, and greed—as he brings to life men and women from his city of Florence and characters from ancient history and myth. He is the author and major player in his epic poem, listening to stories of deep pain and confusion, yet never denouncing the ignorance or lack of morality that brought about the suffering. I don't think he considered human beings inherently evil, and this put him at odds with the harsh Christian hierarchy of his times. *The Divine Comedy* is the revolutionary work of a progressive mind that looks at man's relationship to such realms as Hell, Purgatory, and Paradise, written from the tender heart that adored Beatrice, and in the vernacular of Dante's people, so that all citizens of the land might read it.

I walked across the solid Ponte Vecchio over the Arno a lot during my year in Florence, with its small elegant shops selling precious gold and coral and amber, and I often imagined a small gang of Renaissance painters—Massaccio, Da Vinci, Piero della Francesca, and Botticelli—sauntering along behind me in paint-spattered tunics. Dante was never far away either. I seemed to have my feet in two worlds. My head was filled with these characters—Dante with his love for Beatrice, Da Vinci and his Mona Lisa—as I cherished my blue-eyed beau whose delicate features suggested a young prince dressed in black velvet with white ruffles at the neck. Did he ever say he loved me? I wonder. What did we say to each other? I don't remember any of our conversations during those afternoons together. We were so very shy; we held hands as we walked side by side through the ancient, gritty streets, with little attention to where we were going, until we found ourselves in front of a bright sweet-smelling fruit stand, and he splurged on a yellow peach to share in the late afternoon. These little moments were like images from beautiful paintings.

Before I arrived in Florence in 1956, I had never experienced anything ancient in my life, and walking the cobbled alleys taught me about old: the musty damp grayish smell, even in summer, all the passages dark and maze-like, and then the grand tall arches and elegant wrought iron lamps. Florence's solid stone buildings were like formal straitlaced businessmen with not so friendly faces. Old and dark and forbidding. I loved it all from the start. There were many streets in the center that never saw the sunlight, and there was moldiness in the air even in summer, once in a while punctuated by the sugary-smelling *pasticceria* (bakery) where brioche, marzipan, and brightly colored tarts were proudly splashed across the window display, or the noisy cafés where bitter coffee filled the air. Italians believed in pausing, I noticed, whether it was for *caffè* and a smoke or a little lie-down in the afternoon after lunch. This way of life was so much like a dance: rush and hustle, pause and converse, eat and drink, rest well, and then join the parade again on the street.

I have returned to Florence half a dozen times in the ensuing years and found that magic transparency missing. I looked for those places where some sensory experience, some smell or flash of light on the edge of a building, some dark interior would take me back—perhaps a visit to the convent of San Marco where Fra Anglico's luminous blue frescoes shone, or the long wooden galleries of the Uffizi.

As a traveling friend and I trekked the narrow snaking streets on our way to some church or other one summer about eight years ago, I fell into dreaminess, a memory struggling to form that would bring back my twelfth year: burnt espresso in the air, the scooter exhaust, roasting meat with rosemary, golden light reaching down and blessing an arched doorway, a cloud of cigarette smoke, as children scurried along with their soccer ball, and a dark-robed priest walked purposefully with his head down. Finding those doorways to the past seemed futile, perhaps because I tried too hard and wanted it too much. I wanted to fall in love again in present time with this cramped haughty city, or perhaps I wanted to feel what it was like to be loved by a young man who looked like he had stepped out of an old painting. But I should have known better: Florence is an Italian city very few people these days associate with romantic love. It is a buttoned-up, ladies-in-sensible-suits town that teaches you all you need to know about the Renaissance, the refinement of the Italian language, and where you can get a steaming bowl of *ribollita* and perhaps a decent *bistecca alla fiorentina*, if you're lucky. No clues on how to find love. But how often do we hunger for love in exactly the wrong places?

At the end of one full school year, we said good-bye to Elda and our neighbors across the road and to our little red Fiat. I wrote one last love note to Michael promising I'd stay in touch, and then we packed up and moved to Rome. I don't remember my parents telling me the reason, but I had a hunch that this conservative city was too quiet and predictable for my mother, and when she found an international school for me in the big city that my two grandmothers would pay for, she made up her mind to travel.

I felt disappointed and sad; I had actually settled into Miss Barrie's cozy world, felt deep camaraderie with Elda, and was engrossed in chronicling my young-girl adventures as visions of ongoing love danced in my head. Elda hugged me and promised, with tears in her eyes, she would come down to Rome to see us—"*Ci vediamo, sai, ci vediamo a Roma, son sicura*"—We will see each other soon, in Rome, I'm sure we will—but I doubted this would happen. When faced with the sadness of letting go, we are compelled to make promises we cannot keep: to write, to visit, to hold on, to love, and to remember. . . .

In the steamy late summer, as the soft rolling Tuscan hills and cypresses melted into the flatter, less interesting landscape of central Italy outside our train windows, I tried not to mope, and I watched as my mother chattered excitedly about going to Rome, waving her cigarette in the air, and Raymond remained quiet, his head stuck in a Henry James novel. Once more I had to learn about the letting go and moving on, and I now shifted my attention inward toward that authentic hungry little self that hung out in the shadows.

Two: Beauty and Pleasure in Paris

"Masterpieces . . . are knowing there is no identity and producing while identity is not. . . . If you do create, you do not remember yourself as you create."
—Gertrude Stein

What excites me most about visiting Paris? Those feminine soft-boiled eggs perched in pristine little white cups, *café au lait* and gold flaky croissants for breakfast, a cheesy *croque monsieur* and glass of rosé for lunch, or the brilliant pink sorbet after dinner? Yes *and* no. For a food lover like myself, there are few matches for this city, where individual lives unfold around the preparing and consuming of excellent food. France's culinary traditions are legendary and seductive, this is true, and I am a foodie, but I believe what I really travel to Paris for is to stare at exquisite nineteenth-century paintings, grand old churches and palaces, and wander the damp streets and quays along the Seine (are the streets of Paris always glistening with dampness, or is that only in the old movies?) accompanied by the city's literary and artistic ghosts.

Monet's Water Lilies

I was on holiday that summer with my daughter Sara and her tribe of four—a lanky tentative husband and three children ages eight to sixteen—and I'd had the sense to rent a little apartment on the Ile St. Louis for the two weeks so we could explore the city free of hotel constraints and expenses. On a drizzly gray afternoon, when walking in the Tuilleries felt inhospitable, my young family decided to head off for the Eiffel Tower, and I happily stepped into L'Orangerie, the spacious and light-filled museum that houses the "Nympheas," Claude Monet's giant water lilies that he bequeathed to France late in his life.

When you enter these bright galleries, it feels as though you're walking into a chapel, where a bow and a prayer for Art are in order. I confess to making an internal bow of my own before I feast on these vast paintings, some of them over thirty feet long, canvasses that completely fill the walls in two rooms of this museum. These paintings bring to life the luscious purple-green landscape of Monet's place of refuge in Giverny, a small country home where he tended a vast garden of flowers and trees and lily ponds, built a perfect little Japanese bridge, and where he worked at his Art; the flowers and watery landscapes surrounded him and became a major theme throughout his creative life. He planted a riot of flowers in pinks, oranges, reds, and purples, great numbers of wispy willow trees, and beautiful stately green bushes of all kinds; he cooked for his wife in a bright blue-and-yellow kitchen; and he worked and worked and worked.

I went twice to L'Orangerie the last time I visited Paris, and each time I breathed deeper and understood a little more about the human drive to create beauty in order to survive life's challenges. I slowed down, sat on the wooden benches in each of the galleries, and stared into the lily ponds on canvas, the purples and blues shimmering, the greens popping up cheerfully, and the enormous panoramas pulling me deeper, as though with minimal effort I might slide into this water and swim away. As visitors weighed down with cameras and guidebooks marched and murmured in front of me, I simply sat, staring at the lilies in the water.

"I've never seen paintings so big, Adella!"

Stand back, I wanted to say, *stand away and see the whole thing; this appears abstract, but it all becomes clearer when you step away!*

"Honey, when are we going to meet them for lunch, did you say? Boy, my feet are killing me!"

For God's sake, why don't you look at the Art? I wanted to say.

"Do you think we'll have time to get to Giverny?"

If you don't go, you'll miss the whole point of all of this, can't you see?

"Damn, I've lost my map."

Oh, please pay attention, I implored silently. And then, of course, I remembered that not everyone sees the museum of art as a temple. I needed to be more patient.

Bits and pieces of others' lives wafted about me as I sat meditatively for an hour or more, writing in my journal and staring at Monet's world of water and flowers, noticing the gently applied paint on canvas, light purple gently smoothed on as though patting a cheek, applying just a hint of lavender rouge to a loved one's face. The series of tiny applied strokes felt to me like affectionate caresses from Monet's brush. This man loved his work. I remembered an evening, many years before, in Paris when my artist lover, who was a painter, wept over our candlelit dinner as he reflected on the huge heart and tireless work of Monet the artist, who labored without resting through his late seventies over what he called the "Grandes Decorations," persevering through the long dark years of World War I, and finally bequeathing the eight giant canvasses to the French government following the armistice. Gifts from his heart to his suffering proud country.

Great artists are spiritual practitioners who forever question their relation to the universe and the divine. Monet's paintings, whether of snow-covered streets, haystacks, cathedrals, or the Giverny garden, show us a life reverently and consciously lived. When I look into the sprawling water lilies, I am caught in a single moment of awareness, and the lily becomes a microcosm of the larger universe. Here realism meets abstraction, and I become grounded in my own consciousness, as well as that of the artist. Monet had a love affair with nature, and he knew deep human love as well. His country home was filled with the yellows of the sun, blues of the sky, elegant Japanese prints reminding us of clear seeing, and worn soft furniture suggesting a person who knew how to care for himself. The giant Orangerie canvasses wrap you in comfort and invite you to float on water. A teacher once pointed out to me that we human beings are about 70 percent water and that we cry tears of salt—we are in fact of and from the water; it is our home. As Monet aged, and his eyes gradually deteriorated with cataracts that could not be treated, he began to create canvasses in a surreal and brash color scheme of edgy yellows and nervous oranges and pinks, but he never gave up on his romance with these water lilies.

Finding Art in San Francisco—1952

I remember the pungent smell of oil paint on her hands when she returned home from art school bursting with pride. When I was about six, my mother, Madeleine Violett, threw herself into studying at the California School of Fine Arts, and was soon swallowed up by the community of abstract painters she worked and studied with. Before long, I was wandering through noisy parties in our little suburban tract home, with the ragtag art school jazz band, jugs of Gallo red, and people dancing the night away in a haze of cigarette smoke. My father and I drifted in a world apart, watching the excitement from the sidelines. Mom was a small woman who painted large and heavy pictures that just about dwarfed her; she rented a studio in San Francisco where she smoked and laughed with other artists, learned how to make her own stretchers, and greedily slathered house paint on her canvasses in chunks and layers. All the artists used house paint in those days because it was cheap, and everyone in art school was poor except for my mother. Somehow, she hauled the paintings home in her white MG and hung them on our walls: bold abstract compositions with brilliant pinks and reds, yellows and blues, and occasionally remarkable zigzag-y black lines darting straight through the center like weird exclamation points. I remember I always wanted to touch them, moving closer in to smell the pigment, running my little fingers over the bumps and swirls of paint. They were texture—so gritty and beautiful and wild—and they reeked of oil paint.

She was a good artist, people said, one of just a few women students at the California School during the fifties, happily surrounded in that messy world by the rumpled, taciturn male painters who taught there. She was gone from home a lot, at some point joining the Socialist Party and campaigning for obscure local candidates with her new artist friends; she wore black turtlenecks and very dark mascara and became a serious smoker. Whether sitting at the dining room table or at work in her studio, I remember that she always had a cigarette in her hand or dangling from her large dark red mouth. I watched her a lot through the smoke, thinking she was really glamorous. . . . I began to notice she was flirting with different men here and there at our gatherings, and though I tried to keep an eye on things, things moved quickly, and it was difficult to fathom what would happen next. My father, on the other hand, kept it simple, hiding behind his newspaper in the evenings, and departing for his accounting job in the city at the same time every morning.

During the early fifties, her paintings decorated our tract home in Belvedere, a sleepy little community on a lagoon across the Bay from San Francisco, but pretty soon our physical scene shifted. I was about eight when she banished my father, her love of him now gone, and she and I left suburbia behind and moved to the city, closer to her newfound friends. I don't remember being surprised by this new move, not the way my grandmother was; the climate at home had become pretty chilly, many late-night arguments, some crying, and my footing starting to feel shaky. She came from a family that dissembled a lot, speaking in tidy phrases that seemed empty when the going got tough (I learned later that the name for that was "euphemism," which struck me as just right for what it meant); she wasn't interested in heart-to-heart conversations with family members.

I began to get used to a number of things at this time: the unreliability of her words, the continuing magic of the paintings' wild designs, being alone with my fantasies and worries, eating frozen dinners, and reading a lot. We lived together in an apartment on the first floor of an old Victorian house in the city, and I had the dark bedroom in the back with very high ceilings and not a lot of furniture. I spent a lot of time in that room, especially when she went out at night and left me with a babysitter. It's hard for me now to recall the particular moments . . . there are just a few stories from this time. The landscape of those years has become its own abstraction, a series of ever-changing blurry scenes, like my father sitting awkwardly in our kitchen holding a highball or Rhubarb the cat, as he struggled to find affectionate fatherly words. I had few guarantees then of her presence across the table at dinner or even during the afternoons when I struggled with my homework.

Inside an abstract painting is a possible journey. I doubt that I knew this back then, but the more I stared at her wild paintings, the more I witnessed the shifting and changing of something concrete, until finally I came to see a more coherent shape or story, something else to think about. I was about eleven when our newly formed "family" left America for Italy—my mother, stepfather Raymond, and me. Once settled there, we seemed to play-act at being a family, trying on new roles now in a civil and careful way. That's the way it seems now, looking back . . . I wonder, were we all just an *abstraction of family?* It wasn't the kind of family most of my school friends had—a lot of drinking, late dinners, and end-less conversations about art and politics—and I kept watching to see what was coming. I gradually became comfortable with the not knowing and the lack of translation. When I tried to fathom the mystery in my mother's paintings throughout the years that followed, I rarely found what I hungered for; I discovered instead my own wild and confused imagination.

She did a good job of looking the part of the bohemian artist, and yet I saw that she was more complicated than that.

Raised in a privileged family on the North Shore of Long Island in the twenties and thirties, and destined for the debutante's life, she now tried to forge a creative path away from entitlement and bigotry, to discover a person she could live with, a beating heart, something she could love inside herself.

In the end, she never found the artist's dedication in herself, the passion and conviction of a Matisse, Rothko, or Da Vinci. She stuck it out for a decade or more, and then in boredom or in fear, she put down her brushes and took up a career of hard drinking with her third husband, Peter, and a small group of intellectual highbrows in New York City. When I was older and people asked me breathlessly about her brief chapter as a painter, I remembered the quirky eloquence of her abstractions and never knew what to say. Some part of me knew that the paintings were good and at times beautiful, but I had also been an only child growing up, who had said good-bye to my defeated father, and waited patiently night after night for dinner to be placed on the dinner table before nine.

The experience of seeing Monet's water lilies and becoming enveloped in that watery world he created was similar to the pleasure I had felt staring at my mother's wild paintings. Similar thick color vibrated—the same dense texture, and all those layers of paint pulling me down into a place of mystery. I saw that within a good abstract painting lay unsettling mystery and freedom. But as I grew into my early teens, I began to grab hold of my own story and shape it with words, not paint. My mother's bold and sloppy canvasses were a gift, one I didn't understand when I was a child, and they prepared me for a lifetime of looking at art, from the ancient, fragile Alta Mira cave paintings in Spain and luminous Renaissance frescoes of Masaccio in Florence to the heady abstract brilliance of Picasso and Jackson Pollock.

Years and decades unfolded as I gradually fell in love with Art. And as I grew in this way, I began to think that I might be an artist of a different sort. Looking at her paintings now, I feel the gift, and it is bittersweet.

Chopin at Père Lachaise Cemetery

When I lived abroad as a young girl, my mother and I used to roam through cemeteries in Florence and Rome, tripping down the cracked stone paths to peer at crumbling gray headstones. "Look here, Mag," she would say, "there's the poet Walter Savage Landor's grave! Do you think he might be an ancestor of our friend Walter back home?"

"I thought we were looking for the Brownings, Mom. They were supposed to be buried here in Florence, right?"

We carried on with chitchat in this way since we both had loved remembering and talking about stories of past lives in old places. I have a wrinkled black-and-white photograph of her posing by the grave of Savage Landor, the sun streaming through the tree above, resting on her in her checkered sundress and perfect dark lips, the lettering of the headstone; she looks girlish and happy, and I struggle to recall the feeling. What brought that smile to her face? Communing with those who are gone, or having an unexpected adventure with her daughter? I have always been drawn to wandering through burial grounds separated from all life's frantic movements, conjuring life stories of unknown people buried below, and remembering a closeness with my mother then that was all too rare.

During that summer holiday in 2012, I led my daughter and her family to the Père Lachaise in Paris, the granddaddy of all the city's cemeteries, which offers a map to the different graves as involved as the map of Paris itself. Parisians have been buried in this little city within a city since 1804, and only rarely do you spot recent additions to this community of souls. The little paths crisscrossing each other are cobbled brick and uneven, and large looming dark trees shade your way as you carefully watch your steps. The first time I came here, the cemetery's main attraction was the grave of Jim Morrison, the troubled American rock star in tight dark leather pants who burned himself out and died here in 1971. Signs were everywhere pointing the way to his grave, and I remember being confused. Why Morrison in Paris? I asked myself. I guess I never paused to consider the question. A famous young drug addicted musician just dropped dead here, that's all. . . . I am sure this grand cemetery held many whose deaths were untimely and dark, and a handful who were not proud French citizens.

On this visit I went straight away in search of Chopin's tomb, leaving my young tribe to poke around on their own; I knew I didn't have a lot of time. My daughter Sara didn't enjoy thinking about death and dying. Her three young children had no context to help them and had probably never visited a cemetery before, and in general this young suburban family had little patience with reflecting on life's dark side. Their interest would very soon lean toward lunch.

The composer's grave is tucked off in a far section but easy enough to find, as there is a perpetual huddle of reverent visitors you can see from far down the pathway. Watching over the grave stands a delicate white marble statue of a young woman, and there are dark blood-red roses in a large vase in front as well as other tokens left behind by various devotees. I found a little love note to Chopin that expressed deep thanks for his being someone "blessed by God with such a beautiful vision." Did the anonymous author once play his music as I had, or had they been seduced by his sad life? Unlike many of the burial sites here, this one was lovingly tended, resembling a tiny Greek temple surrounded by a dark wrought iron fence and gate. Many of the surrounding tombstones were blackened and in crumbling, falling-down condition—disintegrating monuments—reminding me of how invisible the world of the dead is. I wondered who tended his grave so well; Chopin wasn't even a Frenchman, after all. He had been an artist in exile from his homeland of Poland, a frail and sickly composer who had come to Paris to realize his dream, and who rapidly became a cultural sensation in the mid 1800s, teaching upper-class women and performing in their grand salons, often accompanied by his lover, the influential writer George Sand who startled society because she dressed like a man.

I now waited patiently for people to disperse, and then placed myself in front of the monument and stared at the finely carved marble relief of his delicate face with the wavy hair and distant eyes. My fingers recalled a sprawling keyboard of black and white, and I felt inside the haunting refrain from his first nocturne in that great minor key of B flat, whose melody sustains and then moves off and sustains again and lingers, suggesting the vast dim candlelit drawing rooms late at night and women in dark blue velvet and brilliants at their throats. His notes moan: Wait, please wait, the darkness will lift. They sound like the cry of a lonely bird on the river that has lost its mate. I had studied his work for many years and could feel his sad melodies in my muscles and bones.

Slowly making my way back to the entrance to find my family who were now impatient with gazing at the dead, I felt as though I were being watched in that dappled space by some old Lachaise ghosts: Balzac, or Bernhardt, or the tragic Edith Piaf. This graveyard *was* the perfect place for people like me who wished to wrap themselves temporarily in nostalgia, to look back, and back again, scouring the landscape of the past for stories that shine with possibilities.

Discovering Music in San Francisco—1953

The gift of music, including the melancholy pieces of Frederic Chopin, was given to me by my grandmother Dimond, who watched over my young years with unconditional love.

I stayed at my grandmother's house when my mother had other plans. It was a stately gray-and-white dwelling of three stories on a very steep street close to the Bay, with gold Japanese screens and soft velvet couches in the living room, some French and English antiques, and a polished black baby grand in her bedroom on the very top floor. My grandmother Lavinia, after whom I was named—though I've always gone by Mag—played the piano as a young girl growing up in Charleston, and then she studied through the difficult years in New York when she was a young mother in her twenties; playing music seemed to help her navigate this new role for which she wasn't prepared.

I first sat down to play her piano when I was about seven years old. I had been listening to her all the days and nights I stayed in her house, following the rich warm sounds that came from her bedroom, and noticing how happy she was when she made music. I wanted to do what she did, to be her: playing all that beautiful piano music and then feeling the happiness that came with it. I remember how little my hands felt on those creamy ivory keys, a small child at a very big instrument, as afternoon sun streamed in through her window, and she explained the difference between major and minor and showed me how to use the pedal. I wanted to become good enough so I could play duets with her just like Grandfather did.

Before too long, my two best friends and I started piano lessons with a formidable woman named Miss Millette, a proper French lady of the old school who marched about on thick ankles issuing instructions in her lilting accent, tapping us on the shoulder once in a while to get us to sit up straight, and rarely offering praise for our efforts. It took us a while, but gradually we were able to show some respect for her. She wore prudish gray suits and had soft and saggy skin, her beautiful long gray hair arranged loosely on top of her head. She was unlike any older lady I had ever seen, both stern and loving, and her passion for the music eventually touched all three of us. We took our lessons around the same time in the late afternoon each week, struggling to concentrate under her stern gaze, and we all giggled with relief as we left her at the end of the hour, smiling and whispering to ourselves the names of the composers incorrectly as we tripped out of the room.

I met up with Chopin later on when I was in my teens, and though I wanted like crazy to play boogie-woogie, my teacher Wally reminded me that I needed to stick with classical music in order to develop my "chops." First the basics, then the invention and the fun. . . . I wanted to play jazz because it reminded me of a time when raunchy, *plunk-plunk* Dixieland poured from my mother's record player, and I watched as she danced, laughing and carefree, in the dining room at night, and I felt that joy in music was a part of my life. I guess she adored this music because it took her to another faraway time when everyone wanted to dance and drink champagne, and all the women were young, beautiful, and happy. From the beginning with Chopin, I fell in love with his melodic lines that pleaded with me in seductive minor

Not All!

keys, expressing a yearning that I didn't need to memorize. Frailty and impermanence colored his music, as it did his own short life; he died at thirty-eight after a lifelong struggle with pulmonary tuberculosis. The sadness and longing in his work felt familiar to me then. When I practiced his long sensuous arpeggios with my small hands, listening to them stream up and down the keyboard, I felt at home, as though I had just been tucked into bed under my grandmother's fresh clean linens while the foghorns moaned outside in the darkness. My grandmother's musical gift to me eventually became a place of safety and comfort, a place where I could forget my mother's absence for a little while.

Grandmother and her glossy black Mason & Hamlin brought me to music. She had effortlessly filled her bedroom—and indeed the entire gray house on Divisadero Street—with the music of Schumann, Mozart, and Beethoven. Music always seemed to be in the air. When I grew up and moved into a life of my own many years later, and she no longer had the energy and heart to play, she gave me this piano I was supposed to inherit in her will. I again took up playing music, returning happily to Chopin and Bach. Many years would pass . . . and then she died at the age of eighty-nine. In the years following her death, it seemed that only making music on that shiny baby grand could fully comfort me for her loss. She continues to inhabit the instrument still.

My Granddaughter Meets Frogs' Legs

The six of us—daughter Sara with her clan of four and me—plopped ourselves gratefully at a table outside the Brasserie St. Georges off the Champs Elysée with dog-tired feet and rumblings in the stomach. This was Bastille Day, France's grand day of independence, and we had marched from the left bank to the right to catch the grand parade, across the Seine and then supposedly onward to the Tuilleries, but we were stalling out, it had all gone on too long, and the crowds had been so dense that no one had been able to see the glorious noisy spectacle strutting down the grand boulevards; our curiosity level was now at an all-time low, except of course when it came to food.

"I want the *steak frites*, Dad!" Cal shouted, immediately waving his skinny little-boy arms wildly at his father who was staring off into city traffic waiting for inspiration.

"And I want . . . I want . . . oh, I don't know what I want," exclaimed Ruthie, "but please can I have a fresh lemonade to start?"

This was the way all our meals began in this family, with a chorus of "I want!" or "I don't like that!" or "Don't they have hamburgers here?" I had been a grandmother for a long time by this time, and I tried to just breathe and let the commentary swirl by. I had set my mind on some smoked salmon and a butter lettuce salad. As I thought back to my near perfect breakfast earlier that same day at the Café de L'Ile on the Ile St. Louis where we were staying—the pristine white soft-boiled egg in a little pale egg cup, accompanied by little symmetrical sticks of golden toast in another tall cup, and then of course the bowl of frothy *café au lait*—I was reminded that the French do a number of foods exquisitely: eggs in all forms, smoked salmon, salty thin *frites*, golden *sole meunière*, hollandaise, Bourguignon, and of course croissants. And that's just a start.

I sat there revisiting in my head the bustling café that morning, the waiters in long black aprons, the black-and-white tiles on the floor, and the steaminess of the windows as we looked out. There is something perfect about the egg, its beautiful oval form a pleasure to gaze at, warm and comforting to hold in the palm of your hand, the creamy and sticky richness of the golden yolk, so good you must lick the little egg spoon clean. The great food writer MFK Fisher reveals her love for the egg when she writes that it is the most beautifully private thing in creation *until* it is cracked open. Yes. The fun of cracking it open. . . . And in the midst of all this pleasure, the faces of all three of my grandchildren disappearing into their enormous bowls of hot chocolate, their small hands reaching for the golden light-as-air croissants all piled in a wonderful basket. All was momentarily quiet at our table as the pleasure of eating and drinking took over.

When I noticed *cuisses de grenouille* (frogs' legs) on our lunch menu, I had a clever idea. Looking over at my fifteen-year-old granddaughter, Zoe, an irrepressible girl on the brink of everything, I broke through the chatter and urged her to try frogs' legs for lunch. Daughter Sara made a face, and I waited patiently. "Oh, yes, Grandma," she said eagerly, "I'd love to try that!" This girl always spoke in exclamations during that visit in Paris.

We laughed together, perhaps both remembering her past bravery in dining: devouring kudu and wildebeest in Africa, slurping octopus in Italy, even nibbling on sweetbreads in San Francisco. She was a kid who happily took on food challenges. And then, too, there was an unspoken thread that joined the two of us, springing from the moment of her birth when I was in the room smiling and crying as I welcomed her into the world. We had gone on many family trips together, and I had been noticing recently an increased curiosity about the unknown and unusual, and this made me deeply happy in an Auntie Mame sort of way. I couldn't fathom going through life without curiosity.

In my three years as a young person in Italy, back in the "ancient days," as I liked to call them, I graduated from eating the rich and eggy *carbonara* and *stracciatella* to trying brains, other organ meats, squid, and tripe. It had always been assumed when I was growing up that I would eat whatever showed up in front of me, and I usually did, compliant child that I was. I never needed prodding, except some decades later when my expatriate father invited me to partake of a plate of steaming bull testicles in a quaint French restaurant in Switzerland. This was a challenge I knew would be hard to meet. When I was learning my table manners as a child at my grandmother's table, she had introduced me to boiled beef tongue, and I remember thinking that its spongy texture and weird anatomical reality could only be edible if I put tons of the dark raisin sauce on it. My grandmother always modeled a willingness to be challenged, and most of the time I followed her lead—that is, until the testicles.

Zoe, who was beginning to show signs of growing into a young woman, complete with dainty little heels, short skirts over long legs, and beautifully applied makeup, ordered her frogs' legs, as did I, while the rest of the family opted for steak, sausage, and smoked salmon. The frog parts soon arrived with little or no flourish, and I watched as she stared at the tiny pale legs on the plate, all lined up and bathed in golden butter and surrounded by lots of perky greens. In the center of the table we had a large platter of long skinny dark green *haricots verts*, those slim buttery green beans that all of us had come to love in Paris. Then came the inevitable *frites*, springing all crispy and golden from a metal cone with the white paper to hold them. A handful of fries, a small portion of the green beans to accompany the lonely little legs, and she and I were ready for the experience. I joked with her about how people used to say that frogs' legs tasted like chicken, so there probably wouldn't be a challenge.

"Do you think they really taste like chicken?" I asked her.

"No," she replied. "They taste like butter and lemon and salt—yum! *So* good!"

Happy at this moment that I was neither vegetarian nor had any attachment to frogs, I thought, Hooray for her, hooray for us! I sipped my Provençal pink wine and realized that she had learned one of the cardinal lessons of food enjoyment: go for the butter, garlic, olive oil, and lemon. They will make almost anything taste wonderful.

Before I ever experienced the sensuous yearnings for another human being, I felt them for food, beginning at around age eleven when I lived in Italy: thick green olive oil, fat white fennel bulbs, and blocks of ochre parmesan, deep red tomatoes from the vine whose tangy fresh scent stung your nose, dark green chard with beautiful red stems, or oily green olives and brilliant frilly parsley waiting to be chopped. We used to eat fat dark crimson-colored cherries in the summertime, bigger and sweeter than any I had ever had, exploding juicy redness inside my mouth. That early food journey taught me that great food is very simple; it must be from the earth and fresh, and in its simplicity asks to be presented without great fuss and bother.

The frogs' legs that Zoe and I devoured that day at lunch were about as simple as you could get, unobtrusively resting on a white oval plate, slathered in butter, and accessorized with looping dark green watercress. Granddaughter Zoe couldn't wait to add this to her list of the esoteric things she had tried on her travels; she talked on and on about this beyond the point when anyone listened anymore, and I felt sure then she was beginning a journey that could someday change her life.

Notre Dame de Paris

Inside this massive "mother church," people by the hundreds milled about, looking up, trying with every kind of camera to take photographs, only to show up later at the souvenir stand to buy the perfectly depicted interior in postcard form. Whenever I looked up at the light pouring in through those brilliantly colored windows, I believed that I could fathom God, a presence I'd had no relationship with most of my life. The Tibetans and Bhutanese keep their teachings alive in temples and monasteries with painted *thangkas* that show off iconic gods amid the glowing incense, and in our Western churches we have Jesus on the cross, paintings of Mary and the angels, thousands of candles, and stained-glass windows everywhere. For centuries, the holy sculptures and crosses and paintings in glass have reminded the Western believer that he has a place in the divine scheme.

Again, I noticed the familiar musty smell of the ancient churches, as old stone continually breathed its stale moisture out into the air, and then there was the pungent whiff of burning wax—the hundreds of blinking votive candles lit by all the believers and wannabe believers. What is it about lighting these candles that touches this non-Christian? Ever since I sat at the dinner table as a child of six or seven and watched my mother light tall white candles in her mono-grammed silver candlesticks, the warm light casting comfort into the darkened room, I have wanted candles in my life to create ritual, even if that ritual is as simple as dinner on plain white plates on a Monday night. In almost every European and Latin American church that I've entered on my travels, I have stopped to light candles and send out little prayers for my family: my grandmother, my children, Francesca my departed Golden Retriever, myself, and particularly my mother. I knew that she needed blessings, both in her life and beyond. She wasn't a churchgoer, but she loved places like Notre Dame with all its grandeur and beauty, and she was more fragile and lost than she ever knew.

As I craned my neck to look up at the epic cathedral windows on our last day in Paris, I wondered about the stories crafted in the brilliant glass that narrated our spiritual lineage, joining us to all the twelve apostles, the saints and martyrs, the angels, and all the poetic and dark tales from the Bible. I felt a strange sense of belonging in that moment. . . . To what? And why? Then my mind soared, and I imagined floating high in the air, close to those magnificent colored windows, looking down through the darkness at the hundreds of visitors who paced quietly with their cameras and bags and maps, lines and little clumps of beings moving in formation like so many armies of ants on a mission. With my feet firmly planted on the cold stone floor, I heard the shuffling of fellow travelers and the gentle murmur of voices, while splashes of color rained down from above, stopping me in my tracks. I felt unusually warm on this damp gray afternoon—blessed by the rays of reds, yellows, and cobalts—inside this chilly Gothic church, and for what felt like timeless time, my gaze remained fixed upwards toward the heavens.

Underground Beauty

Warmth can be found underground in Paris. I have discovered in the vast world of the Paris Metro a population of young musicians dressed in variable black outfits who give freely of themselves, little string ensembles scattered here and there in the sprawling and claustrophobic landscape who play Vivaldi, Bach, and Albinoni to an endless stream of moving passengers. You see them in the crowded big intersections between the main subway lines, creating cozy resting places where they play their violins and cellos with beautiful concentration, undisturbed by the turbulent and indifferent crowds. In their early twenties and thirties, their faces look pale, but their hearts seem impassioned in the playing.

During a particularly hectic travel day when I was trailing as usual behind my family, I stopped still to watch five or six of them perform. I wanted to remain there until there was time to applaud and smile and say thank you for such unexpected beauty, but the rush of travelers, my impatient family, and the strong cold drafts distracted me. I could tell these young men and women were good; I was able to hear that through the noise of human traffic. I imagined they were struggling young musicians, scrabbling together extra coins wherever possible; perhaps students who worked and went to school and managed to practice in their down time, spending hours in small dark rooms with cups of cold tea. Pearly white their faces, dark hair, and worn-down shoes . . . I could have been looking at one of Goya's or Van Gogh's graphic portraits of the unseen working class, in all its dark browns, yellows, and blacks, as the bleak yellow lighting in the Metro intersection cast an eerie pall on these musicians, offering a touch of pathos.

I looked into the cello case hoping to see a pile of money, but there was very little. Those who rushed through had other things on their mind, people to see and jobs to get to, and I remembered too that Europeans were never drawn to tipping working people as we Americans are, often putting more money than necessary on the tray out of obscure guilt or a desire to be appreciated. I dropped all the Euros I could dig up into the case, aware of my family waiting not so patiently at the bottom of the stairs for me to join them, and then took a few blurred photographs of these young music-makers. The crowd was moving fast around this little oasis, and my people waited beyond the blur. I tucked their CD in my bag and moved down the dirty stairs to continue my journey through another tunnel, to another metro platform with more dingy yellow lights and big frayed movie posters, the pounding of feet all about me; their Vivaldi followed me all the way.

Three: Alone in Venice
in January

"The light of winter is a private light. . . ."
— Joseph Brodsky, *Watermark*

In the dark of night in the middle of winter of 2013, I pulled my long down coat tightly about me against the Adriatic cold and marched onto Piazza San Marco. I saw not the daylight face of "Europe's drawing room," with beautiful women in snazzy shoes, waiters in crisp white jackets, riots of pigeons, and corny string music, but rather an expanse of dark empty space at the end of which stood the proud cathedral with its plump cupolas and now invisible mosaics. A few people scurried about far away, and all I could hear was the clacking of my feet on the old stone floor. It was January. I had just arrived in the city this evening, and though jet lagged from many hours of airplane travel, I wanted to get my first glimpse of Venice in uncluttered form, without the usual hordes of people who camouflage the dailiness of this city. Though technically a visitor here myself, in my heart I have never felt like one, I guess because I had returned here many times as I grew into adulthood to walk these alleyways. This particular winter I had come to witness her stripped of travelers, solitary and alone, and to investigate my own aloneness in this barren winter season. Following the social whirl of holidays with family, I looked forward to meeting my own solitude, and what better place for this than the shuttered down city of merchants and palazzos resting on murky shifting waters?

When I think of this city, I remember two movies whose stories unfold in Venice—*Summertime* and *Death in Venice*—in which the central figure looks for a way to warm an empty and lonely heart. Both Jane Hudson and Gustav von Aschenbach take us on a journey of seeing the landscape of Venice and bring to our attention human loneliness and longing. Henry James' *Wings of a Dove*, as well, offers up a solitary journey as a mortally ill heroine leaves behind London society in order to find refuge and comfort in Venice's dark palazzos and romantic canals. I seem to carry the voices of writers with me wherever I travel. I have walked down the tortuous *calle*—e alleys—eof this city many times and have seen myself as a character who must wander alone through the maze to find ease. What is peculiar about Venice in winter is how different it is from most other cities in Italy that generously offer up food, hospitality, and cheer—even romance. Here it is dark gray and cheerless, you don't hear voices or music ringing out, and you don't particularly feel welcome in the little claustrophobic restaurants you visit. Now you can disappear into Venetian life, feel yourself getting older by the day, slowly aging and sinking with gravity just as the city recedes into the Adriatic, and then forge ahead to find something you have not seen before.

In Venice that January, I saw my experience unfold in

layers, watched myself emerge out of the gray backdrop in full relief: a small female figure in front of a shoe store that featured sequined blue high heels, a shop with glossy colorful masks, or even simply standing to watch a lone pigeon amble along the canal. A series of fully developed photographs became realized in my mind. Observer and observed right there. It all seemed black-and-white that January, despite the brilliant glittering glass in the shops around San Marco, or the boldly colored Missoni sweaters on skinny mannequins in the shiny elegant boutiques. The food was black-and-white too: dark squid ink pasta, creamy risotto, pale white wine, and snowy *baccala*, that tangy salt cod that spreads like butter over bread.

Food and Fur-Coated Women

As I came upon the Rialto Fish Market, I was blessed first with visions of purple artichokes and brilliant red peppers, and plump glistening white bulbs of fennel, sexy dark eggplants, vivid colors declaring themselves in the gray light. Then came the shimmering slabs of silver fish with perky dark eyes, and mountains of crinkly white calamari, piles of clams and crabs, and huge red tunas that rose up like mountains. An Italian market is my idea of heaven, a place where nature's generosity and color seduce me. I have loved food obsessively all my life. It has kept my body alive and my heart purring. This cold morning in Venice, I wanted to mingle with the artichokes and the zucchini, inhale the wet salty fish, and feel at home.

My Canon was slung over my shoulder, and the morning light was a steely gray, perfect for photographing bright colors. I must have taken dozens of pictures of perfect baby purple artichokes swimming in yellow buckets, tasting their bitter flavor in my mouth as I snapped away. The fishmongers were ahead of me, and I could hear the bustle of commerce— the serious discussing of everything from *"Buon giorno, signora, come sta? Sta bene?"*—Good morning, madam. How are you?—to just: *Dove*—Where—did this *branzino* come from, to freshness—*"Quando questo pesce e portato qui?"*— When was this fish brought here?—and then price—*"Ma che! E troppo per questo pezzetino!"*—Come on that's too much for this small little piece! Italians are deadly serious about food, and the transactions for a few pieces of fish can soon become entertaining, even operatic.

Venice's Rialto Fish Market offers up literally hundreds of kinds of fish from the waters of the Adriatic. It is a large covered area that stretches for many blocks, teeming with buyers and sellers, little bright electric lights swinging from the roof above, and the pavement a glistening wet surface where the odd non-working pigeon struts in search of some little morsel. Most of his tribe have by this time convened in San Marco to be ready for the tourist-and-pigeon show unfolding daily. I breathed in the sharp salt in the air, no sour fishy smell, and felt dampness envelop me from the thousands of glistening sea animals.

No one paid me any mind as I wove in and out among the crowd, trying to get the smartest and least obtrusive shot. I took off my gloves to have more ease with the camera and noticed that in this frigid morning air the fishmongers wore no gloves. Their large hands were turning purple from the handling of ice and fish, and their faces were ruddy as beets with the cold. Just as I bent low to get a good angle on a giant lobster, I saw in the distance two ladies "of a certain age" in mink coats. They were done up perfectly, had regal bearing, complete with hats, gloves, and sensible matronly purses. These fur-coated ladies shopping for fish made me take a step back in surprise. Who were they exactly? And doing their grocery shopping in furs? Is this not indeed an odd picture? As I moved closer to make my shot, I realized it had been a long time since I had observed any Venetian woman out in the city going about her business. All my other visits here had unfolded in tourist season, when most of the Venetians we saw on the narrow walkways and bridges were men, dapper and aloof in blazers and fedoras, with quirky pointed noses. Venetian wives apparently spent most of their time at home or closeted away in some shop; they were less visible. What I learned in the two weeks I walked through the frigid stone landscape is that a lot of Venetian woman were out in force during the day, happily walking and talking, at the same time of course, arm in arm as is their custom, their small curly haired dogs tugging them along. I also noticed that the majority of these women wore fur coats, long and brown and sleek. But then again, *it was winter* on the Adriatic.

Florian's and Wandering through Venetian Winter Light

To sit inside Florian's on a dark cold morning is to inhabit a pearly vintage postcard. The antique mirrors, all dulled with fine spidery streaks, are ornately framed in gold; the ceilings show off the parade of Tiepolo-like frescoes of angels and princes. You see a lot of old mirrors in Venice . . . so many were made here through the centuries. Mirrors and water are everywhere, mirroring one another. On my way to explore the Ghetto, I came in out of the cold this morning convinced that one of their expensive little cappuccinos would fill my body with warmth and fortify me for my walk.

Florian's has been a social institution in Venice since it opened in 1721, and it is now a gathering place where visitors rather than locals can take a seat back in time. In the summer, customers usually sit outside at little rickety tables and listen to concerts performed by bored musicians dressed in black, sipping wine at extravagant prices, and eating uninspired little snacks. But in the winter, we all must come inside, and so I did. A diffident older waiter who held himself stiffly delivered my small steaming cappuccino on a silver tray complete with cloth napkin and a small vase of real flowers. We barely exchanged words—he was obviously bored with it all, and I was happily inside my head. The little table was white marble with dark streaks, and the floor a beautifully worn dark wood that creaked when you walked on it. Looking out onto Piazza San Marco, I thought of my old literary hero, Henry James, whose *Italian Hours* reported his many visits such that you could hear the gondoliers singing out, know exactly what the inside of a church looked like, and see just how naïve and foolish Americans abroad looked to the eye of this witty expatriate. His brainy essays had always filled me with a yearning to be other than American and to record the traveling experience abroad with pen and paper.

Displacing my bulky down coat, I felt conspicuous here where everything reeked of gentility; this puffy thing I had bought for its warmth seemed awkward and inelegant. At other tables: young Japanese tourist couples giggling softly, and a couple of tweedy British types with damp pink faces. It was very calm inside the café, as though the director of our little film had decided to slow down the camera for just a little while and prolong the moment. I pulled out a Florentine fountain pen and journal and willed myself to write. What exactly was I looking for? Some insights about this particular journey, or perhaps some tender old memories of my time in Venice as a young girl? I wondered about what my twelve-year-old self thought back then about this magical place. I have been here so many times, and seen all the required sites at least once; do I really need to record my thoughts about them? No, I had a different plan: I would wander the byways to discover what lurked beyond the next little bridge or alley, just that, and to embrace solitude. This interval between Christmas and February's Carnevale tourism was not in play, and all the random visitors were free to explore without much attention from the natives.

Pen in hand now, I looked back on yesterday's extraordinary sight in Piazza San Marco in the softening light of late afternoon: a young Japanese couple in wedding dress posing shyly before a photographer with the grand cathedral in the background. It was bitter, the sun was weak on our backs, the rest of us milling about were shivering in our heavy coats, and this young pair turned and touched each other gracefully in this sprawling square, smiling radiantly and showing no sign of feeling winter's cold. They resembled two porcelain figures poised on the top of a music box, slowly turning, and dancing on and on. The grandest square in the most beloved urban drawing room was theirs for that moment, as I felt a tug of longing in my heart that was made more wrenching by the weakened winter light—yes that extraordinary light that turned our collective presence there into a jewel-like painting.

"The light here is the mighty magician . . . and the greatest artist of them all," wrote Henry James in *Italian Hours*. Light is everything for those who go searching for beauty, for it suggests all this: forbidding cold and loneliness, as well as warmth, joy, sensuality, and death. Winter's light, seeping into the dark gray crevices of the *palazzi* and arches and church spires, pulls you down and inward, while the light of summer bounces back happily, tap dancing off the surfaces, widening your expectation and pleasure.

A Bridge and a Book

The dark pink sunset that hovered over the Accademia Bridge one evening gave me pause, as I started to make my way back to the coziness of my hotel after a long slow afternoon of looking at paintings. I decided instead to wait for the dark and watch the sky transform over the museum and that extraordinary old wooden bridge that arced over the canal. As I raised my camera to capture bursts of pink in the sky, I caught another moment of self-awareness: obsessive picture taker snaps photos of something beautiful and wants to possess it, but of course knows better—or did I? Days pass, the experience soon disappears, and I'm left with only the replica of a moment; we all know these replicas are never as meaningful as the real thing.

At the bridge, the pinks and yellows gradually turned to layers of purples, and then the sky finally became deep velvet blue, as many small dark figures scurried across, and lamps came on in apartment windows everywhere. I turned to leave, and looked up at one such window, a tall window with a single red antique lamp with pale yellow fringe shade. Soft warm light bathed the interior with its tall ceilings, and my imagination leaned in closer. I wanted to enter that room and join the people who lived there. I saw shadows and imagined classical music playing. A little Beethoven sonata would have been perfect just then. Yearning and anticipation transformed into melancholy as I felt the chill of separation.

What did I feel like then? Was it like looking out from my bedroom into the living room in the distance where my mother and father were locked in intense disagreement, looking at them and knowing I didn't belong and was not a part of their society, that I was invisible? Or was it like looking out the window years later as she drove off in her MG to drink and dine with her artist friends? Or like watching my classmates play sports, knowing that I was too bulky and too clumsy to be a part of it? When I had experienced this unnatural schism long enough, I became convinced I was an outsider and belonged somewhere *apart*. Gradually I persuaded myself that I enjoyed this life of the solitary observer, a wanderer through life like Joyce's Leopold Bloom, who made a career of being the kindly, intelligent witness to life who was always *other*. Given enough repetition, we convince ourselves of almost anything, I suppose. There is a certain protection we gain by staying separate, Leopold and I, a shielding against the chaos and pain of human relationship. In the epic *Ulysses*, Mr. Bloom padded through one day of his life in Dublin, moving in and out of turbulent encounters and living in his own mind, much the way I took refuge in mine. It's no wonder I loved this character so. He had a lonely wisdom and quirky humor, he was an outsider and a *good man* . . . and how I had always wanted to be good!

Sometimes my brain saves me from disappearing into the old sadness and reminds me that we all walk and live and die alone no matter where and how we travel. Who was the writer who wrote, "No man walks alone," or is the correct line really, "No man is an island"? And what about Kipling's famous line about the cat, the "wildest of all the wild animals," who "walked by himself, and all places were alike to him"? And why is my mind so often filled with these disparate fragments from literature that suggest different truths? It is better to welcome all that comes without worry or judgment. This is our ongoing lesson. And besides, I had a hotel room waiting for me and a soft bed to rest my tired body on, and there would be plenty of warm light where I was going.

The Winter Cold and Remembering My Manners

I don't think I have ever been as cold as I was that January in Venice when the damp Adriatic got into my bones through every single layer of clothing. I'm not sure if the sun ever came out during those two weeks, and the weight of grayness was as palpable as the rank smell of the greenish-black waters in her canals, through which long awkward working boats chugged, and over which the persistent pigeons swooped while the gondoliers, in their puffy black jackets, waited here and there for phantom customers. No, this was not the time for a gondola ride, and I was not the right person. A woman traveling alone certainly doesn't need to be serenaded in one of those long black boats. I was free to march past these young men as I tried to find my way to the tucked-away Fortuny Museum of Design, which turned out to be closed because we were in the magical tourist lull, *le vacanze*, as they called it. As I passed a *cichetti* (wine and tapas) bar with its windows all steamed up and warm looking, I wanted to pause and get out of the raw air. In my Michelin Man coat, I could still feel the air travel up from the old stones and settle into my legs in warm tights. Was it time for a cappuccino or perhaps a glass of grappa?

I summoned determination and forged ahead, though I wasn't convinced where I was headed. I used to laugh and say to my fellow travelers, family, and friends, "It doesn't really matter, this getting lost in Venice, you know . . . how lost can you actually get? How scary can it actually be? Letting go of directions in this maze of circles is part of the Venetian experience." I said this often to my family and friends who were determined to figure out Venice by looking at the map, only to discover some unplanned magic like an exquisite mask store or antique vendor when they could no longer decipher the city map! Eventually, most people realize that the journey through this strange city is not a linear one. On this particular trip I wasn't sure I wanted to get lost, though I did trust I could get from my starting point to the northern part of the city to visit the old Ghetto district that I had never seen. That Venice had relegated the Jews to a ghetto as far back as 1516 was both deeply mysterious and compelling to me, with my rather limited vision of European anti-Semitism. I wanted to walk through the narrow and dark streets of this small tucked-away city within the city—the oldest ghetto in Europe—where ancient faith and tradition lurked, to see a very different unfolding of life, far from the glitz and glamour of San Marco, though I knew the trip would take me through many more gradations of gray: alleys, bridges, and porticos that smelled like stale pizza and urine.

Having taken some strange turns without knowing, I came upon a yarn store that my knitting friend back home had told me about. It was brightly lit, colorful, and warm looking. I gratefully opened the door to a bell's jingle, and the blond signora sung out, *"Buon giorno!"* I have a sensual hunger for yarns that verges on craving, the way I do for fat yellow lemons, purple artichokes, and the earthy bouquet of a crimson Sangiovese, and my senses were instantly ready to be gratified. I then remembered the *non toccare* rule in Italy, that commandment to look and *not touch* that is true in the marketplace, the clothing store, and card shop. The array of sparkling and fuzzy balls of yarn that lay before me in this woman's tidy little cubicles invited me to reach out and fondle, but I refrained, waiting to speak to her about some black-and-metallic jewel-like skeins in front of me. She finished with her other customer and turned her attention my way. In perfectly correct Italian, I asked the question I needed an answer to, and she warmed instantly and said, *"Avanti, signora . . . prego. . . ."* sweeping her lovely slim arm in the direction of the yarns, inviting me to delight in all the beauty there. The door was now open to me.

In the landscape of Italian and French commerce, there is a distinct protocol that visitors must respect, and it includes a number of unwritten rules. Many years ago, when I was trying to negotiate a long-term visitor's visa in the medieval town of Gubbio, I was told I had to complete many pages of application, produce different arcane personal documents, stand in a couple of different lines at very particular times of day, all to make legal the continuation of my stay in Italy for six weeks. I dutifully complied. It turned out I was never asked to produce this official document, which I had thought might be the case. Italians, despite their indisputable charm, manage to make foreigners—those of us who are "other"—crazy with untranslatable bureaucratic rules about everything from how and when to wait at the local bank, properly wrap a package to mail, or pay a phone bill at the local office. Just when you thought you understood the rules, they changed. You go to the bank at a time it is supposed to be open, and a uniformed guard informs you officiously, *"No, è chiuso"*—closed. Why, you wonder? There is a great dramatic shrugging of shoulders and a smirk, and you're informed the schedule had just been changed, and it didn't matter that you were out of cash and desperately needed to exchange your dollars. *"È cosi, signora"*—that's the way it is, madam—they say, flashing an adorable smile. You smile, maybe, and say, "Of course, I understand," but you don't really, and you retreat in frustration.

In the knitting shop, I politely and self-consciously did my part in the dance and was allowed a relative freedom of pleasure in the woman's domain. I left the signora with a sack full of delicious yarns, some with sparkles throughout, some with flower details that resembled cake decorations; visions of the perfect little scarf and hat for my granddaughter danced in my head, now warm and fuzzy with pleasure. I was ready once again for the cold and solitude out there on the walkways.

Lonely in San Francisco—1955

She was going out again tonight, and that afternoon after school as she darted out to the store, she'd asked me if I'd like chicken or turkey TV dinner. I really didn't care, and mumbled, "It doesn't matter, Mom." Those stingy little portions in the different compartments of the aluminum trays were all alike, whether it was sickly brown gravy over turkey, or watery carrots and peas with the chicken. I would much rather have had homemade spaghetti with lots of cheese, or a roast chicken all greasy with olive oil and rosemary, tasting like something alive. Tonight, one of the tired babysitters from the agency came, and she warmed up my TV dinner and delivered it to me on a tray in my bedroom, then retreated to the living room to read her movie magazines for the rest of the evening. I sat there alone on my four-poster bed with my books and the aluminum tray. I put the food in my mouth because having something inside me was better than the gnawing hollow feeling I had most of the time. I was hungry a lot back then. It seems that offering ourselves any nourishment affirms that we in fact exist, that we are taken care of. Raising the fork to my mouth, I felt a wave of numbing loneliness, and I ate more quickly to keep away . . . what? Tears, or just a vast boredom.

My mother and I had always had a problem with boredom. . . . Whenever I said to her, "Mom, I'm *bored*," she would reply imperiously, "My dear, don't you know that *only the boring are bored*?" She seemed to think that was clever, but it always left me with the feeling that I was an uninteresting little girl she didn't want to get too close to.

"You don't want to be boring, do you?" she would ask, as though instructing me in the proper way to be. And waving her cigarette about, she continued with, "You know, you could use more humor, my dear—eyou're far too serious for your age!" There were so many times I wanted to tell her I didn't see much in our lives that was funny, that I couldn't pretend that it was all good, but I had to be very careful about irritating her with my truth-telling.

At the age of eight and nine, I read books, made drawings, snooped in her dresser drawers, and snacked on Three Musketeers bars that I hid in my desk drawer, as I traveled the lonely landscape of boredom. Now I looked over to Rhubarb, our Siamese cat, for some affection and company, but he wasn't having any of it; he adored *her* only, and he stalked from my room to stretch out on her bed for the evening. It was clear that my two little green turtles swimming in their shallow bowl couldn't offer me much companionship, so I decided to look through Mom's dresser drawer again.

Leaving behind my dried-up dinner, I grabbed a chocolate bar and went to her bedroom. The scent of lavender floated up as I opened the top drawer, and I stared at the array of intimate clothing: soft silk white gloves, pink cotton panties, and assorted stockings, and beneath that some pearls, a gold pin that had been my grandmother's, and a little compact with a mirror. But there was more: a tarnished silver cigarette case engraved with her initials, an old wallet, and even an old shopping list, with some phone numbers urgently scribbled on it. What was this about and why had it been saved? Why the white gloves? I couldn't remember ever seeing her wear them—must be part of another time, I thought. It smelled sweet and powdery, and I felt closer to her now.

I often read Nancy Drew mysteries until I was too sleepy to stay awake and crashing into sleep felt good because it meant I wouldn't worry anymore about when she was coming home. I kept the bedroom door cracked a bit because complete darkness at night made me afraid—it had always made me afraid. Time passed slowly in the dark, it was lonelier then. As I finally drifted off, I could hear faint sounds of the radio coming from the living room where Mrs. Jones's plump body was propped up in an armchair reading. I was grateful for gentle sounds in the darkness.

I didn't have many friends when I was in fifth and sixth grade—one special girlfriend, Susan, who didn't go to my school and so I saw her less than I wanted to, and besides she lived a long bus ride away; and one guy friend, José Greco, dark-skinned and cute and shy. He walked with me to and from school as we both complained to one another about our despised sixth-grade teacher, Mrs. Love, with the big bosom and long red fingernails.

One of the things I was drawn to then was going to the movies alone. On weekends I walked down the Green Street hill to Washington Square to the Palace Theater, paid twenty-five cents, and settled into the darkness to watch *The Man with the Golden Arm*, or some other serious movie. I remember that *The Man with the Golden Arm* was a big favorite of mine. Some grim story of a drug addict's decline and loneliness—a foreshadowing perhaps of my own confused relationship with addiction when I was a teenager. Escaping into the dingy darkness was a treat for me. I ate popcorn and Junior Mints, and for just a while forgot how lonely and weird my life was. I bet I was the only kid in sixth grade who lurked in the movies alone on Saturday afternoons, and I liked that. I loved feeling different from others, different and smarter and more grown up. Another great attraction in North Beach, the village-like neighborhood we inhabited in San Francisco in the mid-fifties, was City Lights Book Store, and I would set out on walks there, to wander among the endless shelves of freshly printed paperbacks. After my mother married Raymond, an intellectual loner, he would sometimes join me on my journey. We browsed among other bookish people who walked softly across the old creaking wooden floors. The place was special, a world away from the other one I lived in, and it smelled delightfully of printer's ink and stale cigarettes.

Much of life back then unfolded either in my room or on the periphery of my family as I watched and waited. I was invisible as I lurked patiently in the grownup landscape. I ate chocolate, read books, and dreamed about being someone else or living in a different family. I discovered, when I grew up and studied European literature, that I had a lot in common with young female characters who lived on the periphery, who were plain and stood alone in doorways like Jane Eyre, or dreamed impossible dreams like Emma Bovary. I wonder, did I ever think about the social inequality and the isolation of women who for centuries couldn't fit into the approved roles of duty and invisibility? From the age of nine or ten, the aloneness I felt gradually became normal; it was just the way things were, and I became less and less able to understand the strong feelings inside me that came and went. Dissociation, I think it's called. I eventually stopped declaring to my mother that life was "unfair," and began adapting to a life in the shadows.

I did find a few ways to feel okay. I had chocolate bars, pen and paper, good books, and most of all the watchful love of my grandmother Dimond, who looked over me and showed me courage and good manners. She was my larger-than-life fairy godmother who taught me piano, dominoes, the cultivation of a good mind, and the joys of traveling the world. I had that and the warm busy life in my friend Sue's home on Union Street, where her Italian mother fed me, laughed a lot, and always looked at me with love. I dreamed of being a part of this family, because I felt normal and safe with them. There I was seen and loved *just as I was.*

Torcello

On my next-to-last day in Venice, I took the water bus from San Marco to the quiet little island of Torcello, which made for a few interesting stops on the way. First the boat paused at Murano, the ancient capital of glassmaking, where the huge furnaces were originally built in 1291 so the residents of Venice would not be endangered by fire. For centuries, it was the center for the manufacturing and marketing of glass on a grand and lucrative scale, with everything colorful available: artful goblets, mirrors, vases and figurines, extraordinary beads, and gaudy chandeliers. People with remarkable talent would be folded into the larger system of manufacturing to create unusual luminous beads or lamps, mirrors or vessels, all of which would be traded around the world. Venetian beads eventually became as precious as currency, used on all the trade routes to buy and sell and make men prosperous and powerful. Today group tours are ushered to a couple of the main factories on Murano, given one glass-blowing demon-stration, and then directed to a showroom filled with shelves of monotonously generic-looking glass products. These days, the truly creative artists here are hard to find.

Following Murano, we stopped at Burano, famous for lace making of all kinds, and for the many rows of brightly painted houses that resemble a stage set. The brilliant blues, reds, yellows, and pinks stand proudly along the tiny canals; it is meticulously clean and quiet, and I always wondered where all the citizens were. It would have looked unlived in if it weren't for all the perky painted boats moored along the canals, filled with fishing gear, rubber boots, hats, and bottles of water. Our boat then chugged on to desolate Torcello, a community with a much more ancient history than Venice, and home to the quiet little tenth-century Basilica di Santa Maria Assunta with its soulful gold Byzantine mosaics.

I followed the walkway from the boat along with a handful of foreigners like myself, as we braced ourselves against a damp and howling wind. There is something haunting about this community of Torcello, once vibrant and now dormant. Few houses, a single restaurant, stretches of light green reeds and trees that looked like willows, and then the little piazza with the church. Lots of gray sky and cold, cold wind. A quiet and lonely place where the passing cries of birds and swaying wispy old trees lend no comfort. Once inside the church, the musty chilled air surrounded me, and smoky frankincense tickled my nose. A few other visitors whispered to each other as we all walked the cold stone floor of this silent place.

Looking up at the burnished surface of the mosaics of Mary and Jesus spread across the great dome and the main altarpiece, I felt a sneaking happiness and gratitude for this ancient expression of faith. This huge painting in millions of pieces of gold glass proclaims the magnificence and the humanity of Christ and invites our openheartedness. I have always loved the long, mournful Byzantine faces, whose stare is both sad and blissful, the bold and stylized outlining of the bodies, the oversized dark eyes and presence of a devout soul. I think of mosaics and stained-glass windows in the same way—they both tell sacred stories and are extraordinary in their attention to minute detail and in the loving quality of their craftsmanship. I wonder about the meditative patience and reverence that are integral parts of this work.

Art is a spiritual practice. I understand this now. I have spent many years making necklaces from old glass-and-stone beads, stringing the tiny little elements in a sequence, following an unspoken imperative to create beauty or find a story. I have come to recognize this process as meditation, as it had to have been for the Byzantine artisans, and my art is infused with love. I have traveled to this country many different times and have experienced a variety of *déjà vu* moments: exploring the Convent of San Marco in Florence and seeming to remember that I'd slept in a musty dark cell lifetimes ago, walking over the Ponte Vecchio and visualizing myself as a young Renaissance girl thirsting for beauty, or entering the Torcello church with its mosaics and imagining that long ago I was an ambitious apprentice glassmaker who worked here with little pieces of fire-shaped beauty. Have I have sat and prayed or made art here before? The incense of old churches, the smoking candles, the grimy and badly lit paintings on the stone walls, the small dark confessionals, and the old women—always all those elderly women dressed in black—bowing their heads in prayer. I feel I have carried these ancient experiences all along.

As I rode the boat back into the populated, lit up city of Venice, the already dark winter sky becoming blacker by the moment, I watched couples on our boat huddled together for comfort. I'm sure I had a fleeting yearning for a dear one's arms about me and his warm breath in my ear. A young couple facing me asked if I would take their picture as they beamed my way, brimming with happiness. Delighted with their togetherness. I saw a distinguished older gentleman in a dark overcoat and smart fedora engrossed in his book, a pipe balanced in his mouth, and a couple of tired married elders staring out the murky spattered windows in silence. It was then that she caught my eye: a young woman with a big brass ring in her lips, a Mohawk, and very dark eye makeup. She wore a ratty dark brown leather jacket and appeared sad and serious, in a world apart. She stared with deep concentration at her cell phone as the bright lights of San Marco began to sparkle in the background and the boat slowed down at the dock. I saw her tenderness and sadness. So much revealed here, and so much tucked away from view. And I knew that as unlikely as each of us was in that very moment, we did belong . . . on this boat, in this city in the dead of winter, on our own solitary journeys through the days of our very different lives.

"All kids do that.

Four: Burma Pilgrimage

The Bodhisattva of Rangoon

They call her nunnery the "Chinese nunnery," not because she or the women who live and practice here are Chinese, but because it can be found in an out of the way, quasi-slum region of Rangoon that they call Chinatown, dirtier and more neglected than the central part of Burma's major city. Nunneries in this country are more apt to be found in obscure areas, since the work of nuns historically has taken a back seat to that of the monks, who are so visible that they often appear as natural elements in the landscape just like the tea shops and the pagodas. The monastic system here and in other parts of Southeast Asia has functioned as a benign patriarchy going back to the Buddha's time over 2500 years ago.

Daw Aye Thingye runs the Attula nunnery and is one of a growing subculture of female monastics who have committed themselves to offering the Buddha's teachings to their fellow beings, and in this particular case to women on the fringe who have been abandoned by family and society. I was happy when I looked into her shining round little face, remembering that I had met her on my last trip to Burma five years before when I first heard her remarkable story. Partners Asia, the organization that sponsored both of our Burma pilgrimages, composed of about fifteen practitioners and our teacher, had invited her to speak with us as a living bodhisattva, a living being in the Buddhist world who works tirelessly for the welfare of all. She had a powerful story to tell, not only about her own personal courage but also the challenges of working as a nun in today's Burma. Following a grueling battle with breast cancer in her twenties, when she chose a forest refuge and a variety of traditional herbal remedies rather than the usual medical interventions, she took up the role of dharma teacher in her forties, spending all her days teaching mindfulness practice and sharing chants and prayers with her followers. Her recovery from mortal illness had been driven primarily by her daily intensive meditation practice, and she felt a profound responsibility to make teaching meditation her life's work.

To look into her kind dark eyes was to gaze into spaciousness and peace. Her bronze skin was smooth and ageless, her eyes strong and clear, and her smile flickered a little when she spoke to our group in Burmese, slowly told a story about how she met profound bodily pain with deep attention and loving-kindness for twenty-four hours at a time. She described the pain as a storm of fire that ravaged her physical body as she stayed the course, digging deeper for the loving-kindness for herself that she knew was there. She stayed with her breathing moment by moment. Breathing, always breathing. Along with my fellow travelers on this pilgrimage, I listened to her and at the same time to my own breath and felt speechless at the woman's courage. I'm not sure she would have called this courage, because for her it was simply where her Buddhist training led her: meeting all that comes with respectful attention.

We sat and listened to this luminous woman early one January morning on the top floor of her small nunnery, a tall and narrow little building with light filled rooms, as the city traffic blared through the open windows and the heat began to rise up from the street. The story unfolded first in Burmese, a soft language that lacks our hard and jerking consonant sounds, and then in our guide's quiet English as he translated. Six or seven nuns in powder-pink cotton robes stood around the perimeter of the room completing the container. With their newfound sense of comfort and the bodhisattva mission, they assisted Daw Thingye in tending her homeless and hungry Rangoon women, opening the doors wide to these women, offering soft beds to sleep on and food to eat, and sitting with them in silence as they learned the practice.

Because the historical tradition in Asia specifies that no monastic charge fees for his or her teaching and service, she relies, like the monks, on the generosity of the people in the surrounding community for her little nunnery's basic needs, which include food and medicine and tools and supplies such as cups or needle and thread. This communal generosity is called *dana*, and it was one of the Buddha's favored teachings; it is lovingly enacted every morning before noon in all the villages and towns across the country, as monks and nuns walk the dusty neighborhoods silently with their "begging bowls," collecting food and the other basic necessities for life. People spill out of their houses to offer what little they possess: a small amount of rice, some oranges, some sugar or tea or bread. In this way, the ninety percent of the Burmese population who call themselves Buddhist have the opportunity to practice daily the Buddha's values and cultivate kindness in their hearts.

As she talked to us, Daw Thingye was framed by an altar behind and bunches of yellow and white flowers. No art and no Buddha statues. Simple white curtains fluttered against the pale green walls as she led us all in meditation. I thought at first that I couldn't understand her words, but I did. They were all about love and perseverance, about staying the course. The cadence of her voice suggested returning again, leaving and then returning, as though to nudge our minds to return to our body, our center. That's where love rested. Mindfulness breeds love in the end. . . . This had certainly been true for this brave young nun. After we had made our offerings to the nunnery and bowed three times, touching our heads to her shiny warm tile floor, she presented us with little boxes covered in pink and brown paper, and small notebooks made by hand and tied together at one end with pink curly ribbons. From their hands to ours, a reminder of our connection.

As we left this little refuge, I noticed her attendant nuns in pink leaning out the windows and standing in the doorway with large smiles on their nut-brown faces. I loved these small women in pink who made us feel safe and wished us well. How blessed they were to live here, where the doors were always open to those who needed to come into this spotlessly clean, sunny abode with its bedrooms lit up by brightly colored fleeces on the mattresses, this little home that was saving lives and souls every day. Here, Daw Thingye was giving back to Burmese women the possibility of life, love, dignity, and understanding.

An Italian Bodhisattva in San Francisco— Early Fifties

Josephine Landor was the matriarch of my best friend Sue's family, the family I would have chosen if I had been asked. They lived in a beautiful brown-shingled house on Union

Street in Pacific Heights. She was a dark-haired Italian American beauty from the Martinelli family in the wine country up north, who'd left country life to go to art school in the big city and fallen in love with one of her teachers named Walter. He had emigrated from Europe before the war and was rapidly becoming a success story because of his charm, ambition, and creativity. Lurking underneath his beautiful European manners lay a dark story of exile, colored by the terrors of oppression and xenophobia. Josephine had long glossy black hair that fell down her back all the way to her waist, and she wound it up every day in a perfect round bun on the top of her head. Her olive skin was smooth and warm, her face often lit up by her warm dark eyes and big smile. She was broad shouldered, broad hipped, and she moved with a dancer's grace. I remember that she spoke as though she were singing Puccini, with rippling, lilting highs and warm melodic lows.

She adored her family: two daughters Lynn and Susan, husband Walter, and faithful boxer Mia. She embraced me also, as I gradually found my place here, riding the 41 Union bus across town day after day to be with them. She was an artist in the kitchen as well as on canvas, and she produced a continual array of food in this very personal and busy room with the striking black-and-white-tile floor, big black restaurant stove, and a hanging lamp casting warm light over the dining table. The counters were crowded with glass vessels filled with pasta, rice, biscotti, and breadsticks, and a beautiful green fern hung over the sink. Pieces of art hung here as they did in every other room in the house.

Much of the Landor family's life played out in Jo's kitchen. If she wasn't in her studio painting or taking all us kids somewhere, she inhabited her kitchen like no other room. In the morning, she'd bring forth dark French roast coffee, steamed milk, sweet brioches, and always the morning paper to read—I can still smell the newsprint and the bitter coffee—and then the dark red strawberries to slice into our bowls of cereal. If there was no school, breakfast seemed to stretch lazily into the late morning as we munched on more berries while trying to figure out how to do crossword puzzles and watch "our" mother do her kitchen dance. Everything I saw here was beautiful: brilliant red tomatoes lying happily in a wicker basket, little bouquets of fuzzy green herbs in water glasses, crusty golden loaves of sourdough, burnt orange apricot jam with a fancy French label, and up on the counter pale green lettuces waiting to be washed for the lunchtime salad. She was a master of the salad, bringing on the pale green cucumbers, dark black olives, and ripe avocadoes perfectly sliced and generously added to the mix. She poured thick golden olive oil on almost everything. It was in this kitchen I first met the shiny purple eggplant that always made me think of a beautiful woman's body, which she expertly sliced and layered into a classic *parmigiana*, a tradition handed down from her mother. When Walter wasn't around, we usually gathered at the table in the kitchen for lunch, cutting dark hard salamis and types of cheeses I had never laid eyes on before, and of course feasting on our perfect green salad. No matter how informal the meal, we always used soft white linen napkins.

Walter, who had now become a serious and ambitious businessman, seemed to come and go a lot, and I remember that we children all got a lot goofier when he wasn't around. Jo never seemed to mind. She could hold all manner of chaos in her quirky but well-ordered universe. She often made proclamations about the beauty and excitement of food, making the act of eating seem like such an adventure. "Dearies," she'd say, "I know these artichokes, these big green thistles, look frightening to you with all those thorns, but they are one of the most amazing vegetables on earth, I promise you, with all that melted butter, or the mayonnaise and curry . . . you'll see!" It was impossible not to be curious about food when she talked that way. And when she reprimanded us, which was seldom, I never felt daunted because her warm heart was there as she spoke. She was continually amazed at the unexpectedness of things. "Susan and Maggie," she'd call out, "did you both really polish off that entire quart of chocolate ice cream last night? How in the world did you manage that?" Of course, she knew about our not-so-secret nightly obsessions with ice cream, and it bothered her hardly at all. Then would come her gay laughter, and all was well.

I tried to find time with her alone, so I could share things I couldn't talk about at home: my fear of being a misfit in school; how I hated being chubby, clumsy, and awkward all the time; and, of course, feeling lonely and left out. And as I spoke, she held me with her beautiful black eyes and seemed to settle my mind, saying something like, "Mag, you are a divine person just as you are. You have your father's beautiful blue eyes, your mother's kind and good heart, your grandmother's wonderful mind. You are a dear one. That's all there is to it!" She made love seem so simple. And I had a brief taste of feeling good about myself just the way I was.

I remember Jo moving gracefully always in what often looked like a disorganized world, dancing her dance, making art, schlepping us children everywhere, listening with kindness and humor, and cooking all those feasts that went from one end of the table to the other. And she made all of us who sat at her table feel important. Her kitchen was like a spacious warm lap we could all rest in.

Living with Confusion and without Sleep in Lashio

Outside my nondescript little room at the Golden Hills Hotel, the working town of Lashio, Burma, was waking up and beginning to bustle. It was early in the morning, and from my window I could see the little tea stands setting up for the day—low rectangular tables with tiny plastic chairs placed all around, reminding me strangely of doll furniture—and the people beginning to come and gather with steaming bowls of noodle soup and pots of tea. This coming together marked the beginning of everyone's day in Burmese villages: families, working men and women, students, and the odd visitors from the West like me—all pulled toward one another as we started our day. Tea shops were on almost every corner in this town, and the salty smell of soup broth floated in the air, teasing our taste buds. I could see the bell of the pagoda all painted gold behind some ramshackle little buildings—not the grand temple like the Shwedagon in Rangoon, but for this town the center of their devotions, and therefore grand enough. The landscape included an odd assortment of skinny, mangy dogs slinking about, and whole families piled on rickety motorbikes as they putt-putted their way to shop at the central market, a maze of stalls nearby, selling everything from eels in plastic buckets to fine woven fabrics and costume jewelry.

I loved to sit by the window and watch the business of this little place come alive. I was held in the midst of their very real lives. Lashio was a noisy and gritty working town in the northern part of Burma at the beginning of what was once called the "Burma Road"—the road with a long history steeped in hard labor and war that leads straight north into China. This village didn't sport any jewelry stores, museums, or camera shops for visitors, as it was not a stopover on the tourist route.

I think it was late one night and pitch black when I was awakened by a loud amplified chanting bursting in through my open windows. From a deep sleep, I now attended to an unusual language in a deep and loud male voice, and I immediately wanted the volume turned down. What was he chanting? And why? Grabbing my phone that doubled as a clock, I saw that it was almost five in the morning, and I began to feel disoriented. There is something eerie about that limbo time in the midst of a night's sleep, that murky zone of the unconscious; at this strangest of times so far from home, I was being "serenaded" by a devoted monk performing for him an entirely normal task: sitting in meditation and chanting in the town's pagoda just a stone's throw away.

I soon became acutely aware of just how hard and stiff my little twin bed was, and I struggled to turn over and curl into a fetal position so I could sink back into sleep, hoping the monk's chanting would become softer and gentler over time, but it didn't. It would appear that more sleep was not in the cards. I turned on the light, whose anemic rays were never strong enough to read by, and I pulled out journal and pen. Yes, writing would help. Do some more reflecting on the day's events: that wonderful time out in the countryside with the smiling nuns at their orphanage spilling over with happy ragtag kids laughing at the strange-looking Americans.

The devoted monk chanted on, his voice beginning to sound as scratchy as a dusty old LP, his song bumping along hypnotically. Then a pause—and I thought: the end is here. No, it was simply a change of voices. Another monk had slid into the music stream, and I looked blankly at my lined journal pages where I had not conjured a single word. I certainly had a head filled with questions, like: What was being said or asked for, and why? And how soon would the sun rise? As if the lightening of the sky would immediately bring relief from this confusing misadventure. I have always thought that fearful dreams vanished once the sky morphed from dark to light, and I could see I was no longer so alone. Darkness lingered on, however, and the monk continued his droning. And I tried to listen carefully to the sound of my own breathing, and to let go of the idea that I needed my sleep.

Morning light finally came, and that meant showers and dressing and showing up for a trip to the noodle shop, all the while with monk number two or three or four continuing to sing to us in the distance. As our own chatter among ourselves picked up, the mysterious words from the pagoda gradually receded. Over yummy salty noodle soup, someone told us about the tradition of the Buddhist festival days when a dedicated, often unidentified member of the community donates *kyat* (money) to the temple, and in exchange for this generosity, the monks chant Buddhist *suttas* intensively for many days at a time. When one person donates to the pagoda, the monastic community then offers blessings from the sacred texts to the village, and everyone becomes washed in the stream of words and reminded of the Buddha's way. Our little group went about its activities—that day, after noodles, it was off to the country to visit the tribal village of Lasu and listen to their stories. Then it would perhaps be trips to the market, the textile places, and so on, and all the while Lashio's faceless monks chanted on from the town center.

The next night, when I retreated to my modest quarters, I took a few deep breaths and reminded myself to "be with" the experience that was unfolding right outside my window. Taking in the undecorated whitewashed walls and sad little maroon vinyl chair by the window, I kept checking my phone for the time, thinking that since it was undoubtedly becoming late, something would change. (After all, imper-manence is one of the core teachings of this practice!) Surely the invisible monks needed to rest their voices! I then took out my electronic tablet and hooked up my noise-cancelling earphones in the hopes I could place my attention elsewhere, or simply muffle the sound just for a while. Not being a good Buddhist, I thought to myself, taking note of how familiar that judgment felt. There had been a long string of "bad atti-tude" events in my younger life: harboring a dark vengeance against my mother, being a thorn in the side of all my teach-ers, breaking into the family liquor cabinet, and refusing to say prayers or pledge allegiance at school assemblies. . . . Buddhism wasn't that new to me at the time—I had been meditating and going on retreats for over ten years—but my trusty inner critic had a hard time withholding criticism. I selected Bach's Brandenburg Concertos and cranked up the volume. Instead of pure Bach counterpoint in my ears, I felt a cacophony of Baroque violins and Pali chanting pounding inside my head, and it did little to ease my mind, of course. The devoted monk in the pagoda was louder than ever, and I knew then that I wasn't supposed to win this battle.

Why do I embrace Bach here in the midst of Burma? Probably because his music has brought me closer to the spiritual path than almost anything else, except the example of my grandmother's life and the Buddha's teachings I have eagerly taken on. J. S. Bach's enormous output of music is a triumph of intelligence and inven-tion, and it has given me order, safety, inspiration, and a desire to believe.

And then there is the matter of genius and invention. . . . "Follow the bass line," said András Schiff, a contemporary master pianist, about the extraordinary Goldberg Variations, thirty short keyboard pieces strung together in a parade of variations from an initial bass line of the opening aria. Bach set about varying his "theme" through the sequence, with his musical lines moving up and down, in parallel, and in contrary motion and counterpoint, all of them offering some different configuration of the original idea. Here is both wild creation and a return to home ground. Was this so compelling to me because the life I had as a child was colored by continuous instability, willful creativity, and my own incessant yearning for some kind of safe and solid ground?

My forty-year journey through Bach's piano music has also opened up the landscape of the divine, as continuing invention and variation took me into territory that felt both infinite and safe. I'd grown up in a world where God had been regularly denigrated, and I had unfortunately adopted a knee-jerk atheistic view of life. In all the years that I studied Bach's music, I began to feel something quite different than I was used to, finding in his notes an unspoken prayer and perhaps a small map for life that made me feel safe. As I began to see the connection of Art and Spirit, I felt relieved. I was also able to imagine something beyond the chaos of my erratic life, and at the same time see something vast inside my own heart. In any case, it was very comforting. In the end, the music of Bach offered me safe passage in a world of shifting characters, disorder, and unreliable stories, and taught me that creative invention might be a path to insight and safety, even joy.

Giving up on Bach for the moment, I began to listen carefully to the chants and felt I was able to follow the train of thought. I heard words that sounded reverent and hopeful. And I joined the experience. I had asked our guide, Mint U, earlier in the day about the monk's words, and he'd drawn a blank expression. He was familiar with the ritual but knew nothing about the words, suggesting they might not be all that important. Another thing he was unclear about, which seemed both charming and normal, was just how long the chanting marathon would go on. "It could be three days, or a week . . . or maybe two weeks—one doesn't know. . . ." Yes, it was uncertain, just like life.

I polished off a cold beer from my minibar and decided to see what it was like if I turned my lights out and floated in the dark with the sound. And then, all of a sudden, the prayers ended, the hissing stopped, and I imagined the monk bowing deeply to the Buddha as he concluded his shift. I waited for another one to take his place, but it didn't happen, everything remained quiet. It was over for today, and it was only ten o'clock. I guessed that there were maybe six hours of uninterrupted sleep ahead of me before I was again picked up by the song and taken off into those strange-sounding words. As I drifted off to sleep in my little cocoon space, I tried to visualize the invisible monks who had been singing steadily since four in the morning; I felt compassion for them and was glad for all the tireless praying and chanting alone and unseen, creating all kinds of merit for themselves and others.

Shwedagon Pagoda—the Temple of Presence

The white marble under my bare feet felt warm from the day of sunshine, and my tired feet were grateful. The sky was turning darker blue as evening came on. Rangoon citizens of all sizes walked in a continuing flow quietly and slowly around the giant bell-shaped *stupa* at Shwedagon Pagoda that shimmered in its brilliant eye-piercing gilt. Occasionally a woman or man stopped to kneel in front of one of the shrines where brightly colored Buddhas sat with brilliant colored neon rays of blue, red, purple shooting from their heads. A startling sight, I remember, when I first saw these flashy figures, but I was eventually told that the wild electric rays were meant to represent the rays of wisdom generated by the Buddha's heart and mind. Long ago he had wandered the dusty roads of India, teaching that the enlightened life has two wings, one of wisdom and the other compassion. I smile now at the figures and feel a part of the simple everyday reverence colored by these quirky, kitschy details. Neon Buddhas? And, no, I'm not in a street market in Mexico with its surreal geegaws, or London where edgy Mohawked heads parade by the old Houses of Parliament . . . I'm in Burma. It is perfect somehow. The Buddha was a breathing human being who lived in the "real world" of everyday, and he carried inside all the messy, disparate elements that I do. All humans express refinement *and* kitsch, the flashy and subtle, the good behavior and the rude.

The visitors to the temple put down their parcels, plastic bags of vegetables, and briefcases, and bowed their heads as they sat cross-legged on the soft white stone floor. I put my hands together at my chest too as I walked by, the voyeur who needs to be a part of it all somehow. Incense was burning everywhere in front of the shrines., on metal trays, the smoke curling energetically upward and tickling my nose. Also, the children came to sit, and they stayed quiet and composed, fixing their little faces on Buddha or the *nats*, the colorful and kooky-looking Burmese spirit gods to whom many shrines were dedicated.

In Burma, vibrant animist spirits called nats drove the people's beliefs long before the Buddha's teachings arrived, and they are honored throughout the rugged countryside, some of them carved into gnarled old trees. The Burmese have always had great faith in fortune-tellers, too, whom they often look to for their wisdom and foretelling about marriage, babies, travel, and their hopes for prosperity. There are shrines at Shwedagon for every day of the week with small white alabaster Buddhas perched above a pool of water, and it is here that the devoted routinely come to make offerings to the day on which they were born; over and over, they bathe

the Buddha's white head with clear water, offer handfuls of white narcissus, and light incense. Whole families gather together to offer their quiet prayers as they fix the Buddha with their gaze. An unusual custom, but in this landscape of devotion, it all felt natural to me. If I had known the day of the week I was born on, I probably would have joined this ritual. Instead, I circled the *stupa* over and over, passing all of them and occasionally taking pictures as I went. I randomly made offerings as memories of loved ones surfaced in my heart. In my own awkward way, I was beginning to feel devotion and love. You can always use more blessings, right?

Everything unfolds quietly in this little city within a city, this microcosm of Burmese spiritual life; hundreds, even thousands of unremarkable, unidentifiable people make their pilgrimage each day with few words or conversation. Their noble bald heads shielded by big dark umbrellas, the red-robed monks join the circumambulation too, keeping their attention inward. Candles burn, incense burns, and people cradling flowers in their arms prostrate themselves onto the warm stone floor of Shwedagon from dawn until long after sunset. This place sits at the center of so many lives in this city, and the people come together every day to weave their practice into the larger fabric of life and to discover some peace and presence.

What the visitor from the West sees on a visit to Shwedagon is what the Buddha called *sangha*, or community practicing together, and it moves me deeply because, like most of my fellow Western citizens, I live a fragmented life within a giant mosaic where the intertwining of heart and mind is infrequent. I feel convinced that this polarizing existence brings about a deep hunger for human contact and support—in other words, community. Twenty-five hundred years ago, the Buddha taught his disciples that human beings were not discretely different from one another, but instead were of the same family, and therefore duality and judgment had no place. Many Westerners are passionate individualists; it is part of our unique lineage and the air we breathe, and when we come to a country like Burma that offers a warm bosom of communal experience, we discover comfort. On occasion we embrace this and *fall in love*. On each of my visits to the grand temple of Shwedagon, I have seen a small and surprisingly well-fed cat or two standby in one of the many shrines and watch the circumambulating people. This is also a temple of witnessing.

Walking down the hundreds of steps and leaving the temple behind, I stopped to examine all the statues, beads, T-shirts, and trinkets being offered for sale, and realized I felt changed. While usually drawn to support all the kind merchants who struggle to make a living, and buy their wares, today was definitely different. Today I would leave without little parcels of beads or incense. . . . In this frozen moment in time, I felt full of love for my fellow Burmese, and that was all I needed. I felt complete.

Young Love on an Ocean Liner 1958

I took my very first voyage on an ocean liner at the age of thirteen, when my mother and I sailed back to the United States from Italy for a summer visit with family. We booked a tourist class cabin—my mother forever trying to be egalitarian—on the *Giulio Cesare*, an Italian liner that departed Genoa for New York in late June of 1958.

Mom and I were sitting on the deck in the late afternoon, and she tossed her head back with a smile as she welcomed the sun on her face. She loved the sun. I don't remember what she was saying to me exactly . . . something about how "divine" it was to be lounging on board the *Giulio Cesare* in the midst of the Atlantic Ocean with all the days ahead of us, and I thought to myself, Okay—wonderful—r six days at sea and I forgot to bring a good book! I saw endless days of open ocean and no diversion ahead of me.

On deck now were lots of dark-skinned Italians making noise as only they know how, some of them waving cigarettes in the air, some telling stories with their hands, all of them in heightened excitement—they were going to America to make a new life. There was a young man in the crowd near the railing across from me who stood apart from the others and looked thoughtful. I noticed that he was staring my way and became self-conscious. "Mom, can I borrow one of your Agatha Christies to read when you're done?" I asked. I turned my face toward the rolling ocean and waited for her to pay attention to me.

"Of course, my dear," she replied with a flick of her burning cigarette. I returned to secretly looking at the group of young Italians. This admirer of mine was still looking my way, his rich brown skin shining in the sun. He wore a striped long-sleeved shirt over his long torso—it looked blue-and-white from where I sat—and he held his body with ease. His hair was a great mass of beautiful dark curls. He seemed kind and gentle. I began to think about Michael Stephens at Miss Barrie's school, and how far away he seemed. He had a kind face too, but he was white as white can be, had pretty plain blond hair, and now he was gone. We had been close last year in Florence, but now were going our separate ways—I was off to Rome soon, and he was to remain behind in Florence.

I thought about living in such a big city, meeting a whole new crowd of people in a very different school; my mind wandered as I thought about the future when I felt a presence close by, the shadow of a tall figure beside my deck chair, and then I looked up into the greenest eyes I had ever seen. "*Ciao, signorina,*" he said. "*Come stai?*" Hello, miss. How are you? His broad mouth curled in a smile, and he lowered his body so he could look me right in the face. And then everything around me began to fall away: the sun on the deck, the ocean in movement, the cavorting of people on the deck, and even my mother now napping happily right next to me in her chair. It was the fade out in a movie, a falling away of people and place. . . . My body felt formless and light, and there was just his beautiful brown-skinned face in front of me, warm with the sun as I heard myself reply that I was well. And then I remembered to ask him his name. "*Mi chiamo Concetto,*" he said softly.

The year was 1958, before answering machines, cell phones, and high-speed rail, before people talked about channeling or worked on desegregating schools, and certainly before I started thinking of makeup and perfume. I remember a few things about those six days I spent on board the *Giulio Cesare* as it steamed from Genoa to New York in the beginning of summer: sitting on the deck in the lazy afternoons, my short legs stretched out on the warm wooden surface next to his long ones; the smell and sting of salt in the air, and no mother present for some reason; Concetto playing his guitar and singing to me. He didn't just sing, he sang *to me,* Sicilian tunes with his mysterious, sexy accent, and some Italian pop tunes of the times, like "*Ci Sei Tu*" (It is You), and "*Volare*" (Let's Fly). When he stared into my eyes and sang, I lost touch with whatever was unfolding around me in the golden afternoon sun. Occasionally he leaned over and stole a little kiss on the cheek, so soft and polite. He knew how to do this, and I began to respond—very shy, very happy. He told me he wanted to become a hairdresser so he could make women more beautiful, and his eyes shone with excitement when he spoke of his whole big family from Sicily finally arriving in America to make a new home.

I see other sweet moments: dancing together a couple of nights when there were organized dance parties in the ship's little ballroom—a small circular dance floor with a funky rotating light shining down. Our time together on the dance floor was gentle and formal. Though he had probably never moved beyond the sixth grade, he knew how to dance beautifully with a woman; it was that style of formal dancing young people learned in prissy dancing schools when their parents were willing to pay for it. I had done that and remembered. While my mother sipped her cocktails and smoked cigarettes with Concetto's brother and friends, we danced slowly together, and he pulled my right arm in closer to create a contained space, and I could smell his tangy pine aftershave and feel his warm breath on my neck. I leaned my face into his blue sweater and felt only softness and safety.

What did we talk about then, can I even remember? Or were we both simply in that zone beyond conversation, that place of pure feeling? He reminisced about his family and life back home in Siracusa—eight children and a mother. Father long deceased. His mother would be the last to come over, he explained, as she wanted to know all her children were settled before she finally left her homeland. I tried to imagine this sprawling family in a tiny flat on Broome Street in Little Italy, a funky slum with lots of pizza places, vegetable stands, and cheap rent. As I shared my own story of growing up an only (privileged) child with a divorced mother, I felt some anxiety for his people and their inflated dreams for success in America. Would they all be able to make it? As a child, I had listened to many conversations over cocktails and had learned a bit about my country's lack of fairness when it came to welcoming immigrants. It mattered not what all the hordes of hopefuls from foreign lands saw inscribed on the Statue of Liberty—"Give me your tired, your hungry . . ." But then I felt the warmth in his large hands holding me, heard the twangy band music in the background, took in the smell of youthful sweat, cigarette smoke, perfume, the sound of popping wine corks, and my fretful thoughts fell away. As I heard him say into my left ear, "*Ti voglio bene, sai? Ti voglio bene*" (I love you, you know), I felt a tenderness and breathlessness that I had never felt before, and I answered: "*Anch'io.*" (I, too, love you). The lights in the ballroom slowly began to dim around midnight, and we slowly danced on for just a little longer. He was eighteen, and I was only thirteen, and we had both just stepped out of time.

That summer I went off to summer camp in California, and he remained with his family in lower Manhattan, about to begin his new American life. He wrote to me devotedly, and his letters read like love songs. I put them under my pillow at camp, and when I got back to Italy, I continued to hold them close, sniffing them to see if I could detect his aftershave, memorizing some of his poetic phrases, and feeling my heart swell with pride. I sent him a photograph or two and waited impatiently for the next letter from America. I went to classes at the international school (name of school was International School of Rome, so I thought it should be capitalized), made a few friends, wrote a satirical play about Americans in Europe, and took up drinking espresso while my mother disappeared into an affair with a young Roman journalist—in short, I started to grow up in the midst of my weird family as my mind kept leaning toward my immigrant boyfriend who lived in New York on Broome Street.

A year passed and I returned home to the United States, and Concetto and I came together again at my grandmother's fancy house in Long Island. When I watched him get off the train, there was an immediate queasiness in my body that made me almost dizzy. And the closer this hopeful young man moved toward me in the bright noonday sun, the more I sensed my tender feelings for him drifting away, leaving a hollow frightened space inside. It seemed that he had moved beyond me now . . . or was I beyond him? He reached out to embrace me as my mother and stepfather stayed back, and out of politeness I allowed myself to be folded into his arms while my stomach churned. I don't remember what we said exactly, but I do recall a strange apprehension I had never had before: class and age and worldliness and foreignness—rall these markers were tumbling down around me. I led him by the hand to a waiting car and what felt like the interminable ride to my grandmother's house. Fortunately, Mom and Raymond chipped in with conversational chitchat, and we glided effortlessly through the dappled green lanes of Oyster Bay.

As we walked into the grand entrance of my grandmother's house, I saw our two worlds fall away from each other, as though a lovely egg had suddenly cracked in two; I was surprised, and I wasn't. Mostly I was scared. Had I ever imagined back in the beginning of our dreamy romance that we had a few profound problems, such as lineage and age? While my grandmother gossiped and smoked over cheese soufflé served on porcelain plates, I retreated to my mother's bathroom to find something in her medicine cabinet to help me dull the panic. I swallowed a couple of tranquilizers so I wouldn't feel the sad betrayal. After lunch, I tried to explain to Concetto that it was over, that we didn't really have a future, and the sinking sad feeling stayed with me. We sat numbly on pretty lawn chairs on the patio looking out over Oyster Bay with its fancy little boats bobbing about on blue water in the distance. As I look back, it reminds me of the pain and confusion felt by Scott Fitzgerald's Daisy Buchanan when she finally understood the impossibility of her beloved Gatsby and cast away someone deeply loved who simply didn't fit in her life anymore. It was chilling, just like that.

Just how I spoke the words, I have no memory of, only that my fluent Italian faltered under the strain of speaking the truth, and I probably resorted to simpler words that never quite communicated my feelings. I managed somehow to draw the line, and he took it quietly and with tremendous grace. Then I watched him get on the Long Island Railroad train back to lower Manhattan, turning around at the last minute with a sweet little wave and smile; how could he be smiling at me now, I thought to myself, after what I've done? My chest hurt and hot tears filled my eyes; I was sure I'd never see him again . . . except in my hungry imagination, the landscape where I would retreat from time to time to be reminded of one rare meeting that changed my entire life. And as I grew up over the next thirty years, each time I spoke of or thought about or yearned for love, I sensed Concetto inside me as a reminder of a gentle open heart.

On my frequent trips back to New York City in middle age, I found myself instinctively heading south toward Broome Street and his old neighborhood, now right in the middle of a glitzy and gentrified district called Soho, hoping to catch a glimpse of a gracefully older, still dashing, green-eyed Sicilian gentleman walking the streets alone.

I never found him.

The Presence of Villagers in Lasu

A number of our group walked up a dirt path outside the tiny village of Lasu in the late morning, bright warm sun shining and bouncing off the brilliant colored hats and vests they wore.

We were a motley crew of Americans (many with Buddhist leanings) who had signed on to travel parts of the countryside with Partners Asia, a brave hard-working nonprofit that partners with community organizers and activists in Burma to build and support sectors of the society that the government has ignored. We were on this trip to visit and learn from a number of communities who were rebuilding whole towns and villages with pathetically small resources. We traveled to see newly constructed pristine medical clinics, to deliver basic supplies to impoverished out-of-the-way schools, and to meet women of all ages residing in AIDS refuge houses, newly built simple structures that were home to many women and children who were living with HIV-AIDS.

On this particular day, the Lasu villagers—recently relocated to this exquisite rolling hills location about twenty-five miles from Lashio—were going to tell us about their way of life and their plans for education and farming and financial stability. We were about as foreign to each other as is possible. One look into their eyes was enough to know they had rarely, if ever, laid eyes on Western white folks like us, and there seemed to be a heightened excitement on both sides as we came together. A large contingent of villagers, smiling cautiously, stood in a perfect line to wait for us at the top of the hill. Many of them wore traditional dress: dark blue vests with extraordinary red-and-green woven borders and hats with neon-colored pom-poms around the edges, while others were dressed in nondescript, well-worn Western T-shirts and frayed pants. Their dark worn hands reached out to us as we approached, and their smiles began to multiply. We held on to those strong, warm hands, and felt their strength and good will. It was impossible not to fall right into their weathered faces with our gaze. They spoke in their tribal language and welcomed us to their village, all the mysterious words rippling over us. The women's faces opened more than the men's, and their grip was surprisingly strong and assured, as their smiles lingered under the surface. The children, on the other hand, beamed widely. I found myself impulsively muttering in English that they could not understand, "So happy to see you, so glad. . . ." or something like that. Clearly, we had no common vocabulary, but we certainly had touch and witnessing through our eyes.

We spent the morning here talking to them about their lives and their dreams for their families. There was only goodwill, and not resentment, when they spoke of the back-breaking work to cultivate the land in this new place, to build new houses, and organize schools for the children, all this without support from their own government. The fact that they were a tribal people in exile in their own country didn't diminish the passion they felt for creating community. Their village leader and his wife patiently explained through an interpreter that their primary concern was the education of their young, and when they couldn't get teachers from the outside (because the Burmese government was unwilling to build schools for the many ethnic minorities spread throughout the country), they set to work training their own. These cherished children danced about on the perimeter of our conversation and watched the white visitors with obvious curiosity. We must have looked so strange to them indeed, with our big sunglasses and floppy hats and pale skin. Westerners don't usually end up here. We eventually ate a meal they had cooked for us in their primitive stone kitchen, and they sat silently and proudly watched our every bite. Beautiful brothy soup, exotic weed-like greens and roots, noodles, and sweet white fish. . . . And when it was time to move on, they sent us off with the fanfare of a traditional tribal dance performed in a giant circle in the bright afternoon sun; we were, of course, pulled into the dancing and patiently taught the steps. As we later walked down the path away from their village, they clustered together and waved, and waved, and waved happily.

How is it we get to know people? Eye-to-eye contact and a silent exchange of thoughts driven by curiosity. I found myself staring back into the faces of so many in Lasu and finding only clear seeing coming back. A gentleman with a beautiful checkered blue shirt and jaunty traditional black cap decorated with wild-colored tassels looked at me so intently that I felt shy all of a sudden about taking his photograph. His weathered face was soft, and a smile played over his lips as I finally got up the nerve to ask him if he'd give me permission to take his picture, moving my camera about to act out the question. He assented, and when I showed him the reflection of his picture on the camera's screen, we both laughed, and then laughed a little more. His eyes didn't grow big with awe as the children's had, but they still told me he saw me and was happy we had met.

A Meeting with "the Lady"

We entered a nondescript little modern home in the city of Naipydaw, Burma's newly manufactured, somewhat surreal capital that sprawls awkwardly with broad boulevards but no cars in the flat, dry countryside far away from the humming cultural center of Rangoon. Feeling a heightened anticipation, we walked through a white metal gate and were shown into a sparsely arranged dining room. The walls were a stark white that showed off one striking square painting of a tree in full blossom, all pale blue and many shades of pink. We sat around the long dark teak table and waited. Beginning our journey at three thirty that morning, we had traveled over four hours by bus to arrive for our meeting with the woman referred to as "the Lady," known to the world as Aung San Suu Kyi. Because we were part of a group (many of us meditators) dedicated to community service in Burma, and because our teacher, Jack Kornfield, had formally asked in advance, she had agreed to a brief time in her home to talk about the current state of affairs in the country. I felt a fuzzy weariness in my brain as bright sun poured in through the windows, but also a little zing of anticipation at meeting the adored hero of the Burmese people.

When she walked into the room, I thought I had never seen anyone quite so beautiful. In a close-fitting, red-patterned silk dress, and wearing her signature flower in her hair behind her ear (today it was blood red), she moved gracefully to sit down with us, a cool, polite smile spreading across her small oval face. It was as though she had stepped out of the painting of a bodhisattva—tall, slim, and serene, loving and unflappable. At first appearing formal in her countenance, as both heroine and politician (she was conditioned to such public meetings), she relaxed quickly and welcomed us to her home. She spoke with a British accent, sitting ramrod straight in her chair, answering the carefully worded questions put to her by some of our chattier travelers. We had been instructed not to ask her about her family, and so we talked about the political challenges in Burma now that the generals in power had relinquished some of their control. We were all hungry to understand how things had changed in the country, and she was cautious in offering the information. As I struggled with my new camera, which was now showing signs of non-functioning, I remember her talking about the importance of educating the vast numbers of unseen, unsupported children in her country, about bringing women into the political and governing process, and of the urgent need for conflict resolution between diverse warring tribal communities, in particular the Buddhist and Muslim factions in Rakhine State.

In this out-of-the-way region in western Burma, what amounted to a civil war had been brewing for over three years because the military government had declared that the Rohingya people, Muslims who had lived there since the fifteenth century, were no longer citizens. An isolated incident had triggered the crisis: the murder of a Buddhist woman in the area by a Muslim. This set off ongoing violence between the local Buddhist and Muslim populations, much of it fueled by the militant speeches of an errant Buddhist monk. To many inside and outside of Burma, this racist uprising felt antithetical to the Buddha's teachings and therefore incomprehensible. Aung San Suu Kyi attempted to put this conflict into context, reminding us that this was just one of many instances of tribal oppression that was causing suffering in Burma, where until fairly recently most signs of disharmony and bloodshed had been concealed from the West by the government-controlled media. Suu Kyi and her fellow politicians needed to build an infrastructure that would provide conflict mediation and restorative justice in a system clearly out of balance, she explained to us. She spoke the right words but offered no plan or sense of certainty that political action would be forthcoming. Clearly there was a limit to what she could share.

As private as she is, there are still some details of her life that have become public knowledge and have kept her alive and well in her people's hearts. There were those seventeen years of house arrest in her lakeside home by a military junta threatened by her influence, a historical period where the mere mention of her name by average citizens on the street could get them arrested. When she was finally released from confinement, Aung San Suu Kyi chose to give up the identity of cultural "icon" and join the political landscape to work for the rights of her people as her father had done. Her father, General Aung San, was a national hero who brought democracy to Burma but had been assassinated when she was only two. The military junta then snuffed out the democratic rule of law and suppressed the National League for Democracy that he had fostered. Given her iconic status, she had always been linked to her heroic father, but it turns out that her primary role model was her mother, who shouldered the wellbeing and safety of her family following the general's death; and for whom "Daw Suu" (the traditional term of respect bestowed on her by her followers and compatriots), many years later, sacrificed family and a comfortable life in England. When her mother became gravely ill, she returned to Burma to take care of her, leaving behind two sons and a devoted husband. When her husband later received a terminal diagnosis, she realized that, should she go to his bedside, the military government would prevent her from ever returning to her native country. A cruel move indeed. And so, she remained in Burma.

I noticed as I struggled with my uncooperative camera that she rarely smiled when sharing the small pieces of her story, the weight of her past choices perhaps still heavy on her mind. She had sacrificed those she loved deeply for her ideals and her commitment to bring justice and reform to the people of Burma. Born of a charismatic reformer, with the necessary political genes in her system, she went down a preordained path, it seems, and for this she suffered gravely. I took note of her beautiful porcelain-like face that hinted at her guarded suffering and noted few signs of her advancing age; she was sixty-nine and looked much younger. "What kept me going always was my Buddhist practice, the daily meditations," she told us that morning. She talked of reading the books that her followers sent her and of her daily meditations, reminding us that mindfulness practice more than study had nourished her. She seemed to have emerged from confinement, not as one who had been diminished, but instead as one who possessed confidence and an open heart. I believe that she prevailed because she refused to allow hatred of her captors into her heart.

The time we spent with her in her little dining room was short because she had places to go and politicians to meet in Rangoon. Time had passed too quickly. I wanted to keep it from ending somehow, to sneak in one last insightful question perhaps. Our time together had been both heavy and tender, as there was so much that had not been said, but in the end we all grinned proudly as we posed for our group photograph with this enigmatic woman. She assured us that her staff would offer us a traditional curried noodle dish for breakfast, and then we could rest and recuperate before journeying on. She seemed reluctant to fly away from us, I thought. Or was that my own heart speaking? Did she want to say more to these tired, friendly Americans who had come so far to see her . . . to continue to spread the light of truth about her distressed country? There was so much the outside world didn't (couldn't) know. And then suddenly she was gone, leaving behind a breathless feeling and a fluttering in our hearts of affection and hope. Bodhisattvas, it turns out, are everywhere—they live on the streets, in the hospitals and schools, in homes, teashops, in the halls of parliament, and in the marketplaces . . . everywhere. We had just been touched, not by some beautiful icon, but by a determined patriot who had learned how to transform suffering, a deeply human woman who cracked open our hearts with her grace.

2018 Postscript

Those intimate experiences of four years ago now feel quite far away, and I find there is more to say about this remarkable woman and her struggling nation. I have not been back to Burma since I recorded those events, but I communicate and am friendly with those who have, with people who are witnessing more closely the turmoil that is raging in this country still oppressed by the military junta. What I have learned does not fill me with the kind of idealism I remember having in 2014. It seems there is much darker trouble afoot, as well as a press that remains in the grip of the military rulers.

The humanitarian crisis of the Rohingya has escalated dramatically in the years since I wrote about Suu Kyi, descending to what most people see as ethnic cleansing. This has, of course, attracted worldwide attention. The inhumane treatment of the Rohingya is tragically not the only form of genocide being carried on by Burma's government. A number of other ethnic minorities, including the Kachin, Karen, Chin, and Mon, are being attacked and abused as the Burmese generals continue to enact their racist policies. In the midst of this chaos, we have Aung San Suu Kyi, once a heroine to her people, who appears mute on the subject of the cruelty. Her reputation as protector of human rights and peace activist is gradually being eroded as people around the world react harshly and make judgments largely based on what government-controlled media have to offer. What many may not know is that the country's current constitution assures that Suu Kyi, as a member of Parliament, has very marginal power within her government. Not only that, but she is widely despised by the generals for what she has symbolized over the years in her country, and this puts her life in serious jeopardy. In spite of this, some observers speculate that she is working in a very quiet way toward coalition-building among a number of ethnic minorities to pave the way for an ultimate change in the country's constitution; she works in the shadows in order to prevent more warfare within her country. She is allowing her once lofty reputation to be maligned, if not destroyed, so that intelligent and safe political change has a chance in Burma. I suspect those in the know believe that if she were to speak out and rally her followers, the generals would have few compunctions about eliminating her and her cohorts.

Silence is a powerful force in both good times and bad. Silence can lead people to believe there is cruel indifference to injustice, but it can also enable subversive and progressive changes in a society. Democracy in Burma is very fragile today. It always has been. Aung San Suu Kyi knew this back in 2014, when we were struck by her caution and reserve in sharing stories with us, and she most certainly knows this to be true now in 2018. What passes for chilly, unfeeling behavior on her part is in fact something entirely different. This woman has had plenty of experience operating in the shadows, behind the scenes—consider her many years under house arrest—and she knows how to work for change without making a show of it. Everything about her life as a young political figure suggests self-sacrifice and a steely steadiness of mind that might easily be misinterpreted as lack of compassion. Despite the swirling accusations and the outrage coming her way, I confess I lean toward the side of trust and faith rather than judgment and anger. I have generally believed the best in people during my life, and I am choosing to hold that same faith in her. If I took one salient notion away from that meeting back in 2014, it was her undeniable connection to the life of mindfulness and non-harming. I happen to put a great deal of weight on this kind of dedication.

There are people who call themselves Buddhist who imprison and kill others. A teacher on my first trip to Burma remarked that these were called "bad Buddhists." And then there are Buddhists who live their lives according to the principles of wisdom and compassion and non-harming, but because of their ability to *abide with the unspeakable in life*, they might be viewed as less than righteous. Not so. An ardent and "good" Buddhist knows that for change to come, the causes and conditions must be right, and it is generally not up to a single individual to bring about revolution. This good Buddhist must remain true to the principles, be patient and trusting, and speak the truth only when it is *timely* to do so. I believe Aung San Suu Kyi occupies this painful place now, and I intend to keep journeying, asking questions, reflecting, writing, and keeping the faith as the suffering in Burma continues, and we all struggle with our deepest emotions.

Five: Spiritual Practice in Bhutan

May all beings be happy

I had traveled such a long way to get to Bhutan, from San Francisco to central India to see the Ellora and Ajanta caves and walk by the ancient Buddha statues and paintings, to Delhi, and now I was flying right over Mt. Everest, getting closer and closer. Many of the travelers on this airplane scurried to windows to photograph it, *oohing and aahing* as they did. Facing the fact that I too was a tourist, despite many years trying not to be, I gave in to the impulse to snap pictures of this legendary sight, sensing both anxiety and excitement as we traveled farther and farther away from what I knew. And yet . . . and yet. . . . The majestic mountain all dressed up in brilliant snow and ice was so close, so feminine and mysterious.

A day later I walked in the pine forest above Paro with my young guide, Karma, and we talked of many things: he spoke of being a monk as a young boy, and of his country's beloved young king, Jigme Wangchuck; I spoke of the Dalai Lama and my years of hopping on airplanes to get to his teachings so I could be in his presence. Karma admitted that he was curious about why a single older woman like me was traveling all alone to his country. "I've become way too independent and stubborn to enjoy being herded about in groups like so many sheep," I told him. "I tend to be interested in unpredictable and unusual things. I like to make discoveries spontaneously as I go along."

He smiled at me as though he understood. He had a small, round brown face with alert dark eyes, and his gaze was open and clear as he spoke wistfully of the time when he gave up on the monastic path as a youth because of its intense discipline. He was coming of age now in a time when tourism in Bhutan was flourishing, and people from the West were arriving in great numbers with wide-eyed curiosity; he confessed he wanted some day to travel beyond his protected land, and it was clear that working with those who came to visit would help him do that.

He looked so smart and capable in his traditional black kilt and sturdy hiking boots with sensible thick socks. Ready for hiking. I reminded him that I wasn't in Bhutan to hike the mountain trails like most of today's tourists, I was by no means a trekker. I wanted to see Buddhist life up close, to go to monasteries and inhale the incense, bow before the shrines and the flags, and continue to ask all my questions. As he watched me struggle to frame a photo of the town below us, he told me photography was a serious hobby of his, and he loved taking pictures, so I offered him my spare Canon and said, "please do." In the late afternoon as the sun sank behind the giant mountains, we stood quietly as the pine trees whispered in the November breeze, and it seemed we were looking then at one another's faces with unexpected familiarity. I made a mental note to ask him about his country's vision of "Gross National Happiness," that extraordinary un-Western concept of measuring a culture's standard of living not in monetary terms, but by the degree of wellbeing that all citizens of the country experienced. A mind-bending concept for a well-off American like myself, cushioned by material comforts and the dissembling of many of the well-heeled members of my family.

We began to look toward the week ahead of us: temples, monasteries, market visits, and driving into the stunning mountains, and of course a lot more conversation. Karma seemed happy at the prospect, I noticed, because he was going to be able to revisit some of the monasteries and temples that had been important to him as a youth, and I pulled on the white kata scarf he had wrapped about my neck at the airport and felt grateful for his undisguised eagerness to show me his country.

May all beings be healthy and strong

Like all other visitors before me, I came in on a plane that landed in Paro, which is where all aircraft from outside the kingdom touch down, a small community nestled in a sleepy valley. It is a village where visitors wander noiselessly among the white houses trimmed in brilliant reds and blues, with roofs that resemble peaked hats; and where women with swaddled babies stand in doorways and fix us with their dark eyes, bathed in a strident high altitude sun, their skin smooth and copper-colored; and where elder women watch us with only mild curiosity, their faces puckered like little brown apricots left out to dry in the sun. As Karma and I walked the streets looking for a store with old Tibetan *thangkas* (scroll paintings), small groups of school children, their skin darkly burnished by mountain sun, rushed toward us grinning and clamoring to have a picture taken, as they stared with the blackest eyes at my foreignness. It has been barely fifty years that visitors have been coming here, and it occurred to me that no matter how normal I felt to myself, I might indeed look freakish to them in my oversized, drab photographer's vest, pale skin, and flashy green sunglasses.

This awareness that I walked through landscapes as a stranger reminded me of journeys in China, Africa, and Vietnam, all cultures where the white Westerners are seen as unfamiliar minorities, where we are being studied as though we were the objects of curiosity, not the other way around! Do we travel to faraway places to learn what "foreign" is, or perhaps to find that foreignness inside ourselves? I loved tweaking my version of this paradigm: that a middle-class white woman is seen as "alien" made me smile and hold myself more lightly. I had been a black sheep growing up, a quiet overweight girl on the fringes of my family, trying to gain respect in many different ways while still holding on to my uniqueness, and being "other" felt familiar to me here in faraway Paro. I paused to show the romping children images of their beaming faces on my camera, and they giggled wildly at the magic before scurrying away into the dusty quiet street. This high mountain quiet felt vast, unlike any landscape I had experienced before, everything stretching out into infinite brilliant blue sky. . . .

Paro was my home base in Bhutan, a simple place without much commerce or hustle. I unearthed a dusty little handicraft shop where they sold dusty mala beads, T-shirts, backpacks made in China, and fancy postage stamps. We found a few dark and unpopulated restaurants that served up wildly hot curries, a souvenir and book shop, and a recently built shiny clean (and empty) hotel. As we walked around, we were often followed by a few dusty slow-moving dogs, there being little car traffic to speak of, no street noise, and no police. There was just a sense of resting in this little bowl of safety held by the Himalayas under an endless sky.

May all beings be free from suffering

Karma and I took several road trips away from Paro, to the Ha Valley, Punakha, and to Thimpu, the capital city, snaking up through the tortuous mountain roads, winding through the pine, hemlock, and spruce whose perfume stung the nostrils. On our way to a picnic in Ha, we stopped at the summit at about 12,000 feet, where a sweeping blanket of prayer flags danced in the wind. Banners of red, yellow, and blue, most of the color now washed out by wind and time, stretched as far as I could see, and in their midst hundreds of waving white flags. "We put those up here to honor our dead, to send the blessings for their continuing journey out into the universe," Karma offered. This riot of flags stretched across the summit and beyond, shouting their prayers into the wind and sky. On one side a drop into the valley, and on the other snow-covered mountains. We were on the highest peak in Bhutan, and I felt a little giddy, as though we were flying free in space like birds or little planes far above the valley below.

The only sounds were moaning winds across the ridge, and birdlike cries streaming across the sky. This congregation of prayer flags whipped furiously, Karma and I took pictures of the view and each other, and I sent some silent prayers out to my family so far away ("May you all be happy and safe and peaceful") and to these gentle people who were taking care of me here ("May you be held in safety and compassion"). This isolation I was feeling here was a benign one. I was alone and saw old familiar images start to fade from my mind, but I knew I was held by a larger community, and I was safe. Up here at the summit, there was a brightly painted shrine with a large prayer bell, and on weathered red-and-green wood I read the words in English: "The greatest religion never gives suffering." Of course, I thought, remembering how grateful I was for my Buddhist practice that taught me the importance of letting go of old stories and judgment, of opening the heart and finding communion with others, and of staying present to all the joys and sorrows in life. The sky was the most brilliant blue I had ever seen, and I felt my heart stir. I was standing between heaven and earth.

May all beings be peaceful

The Drakarpo monastery hangs off a cliff above Paro—this location was one of several chosen in the seventh century by the legendary Padmasambhava, fondly called "Guru Rinpoche," Bhutan's primary hero who was believed to have brought Buddhism all the way from Tibet riding on the back of a flying tigress! The little kid in me, who had basked in all the Greek myths my grandmother read to me and thought that the stories of transformation in Kipling's *Aesop's Fables* were magical, loved this piece of Bhutanese lore. Perched right on the edge of a mountain, this place looked ancient, solid, and welcoming. A simple white structure literally hung out in space and was topped with the characteristic hat-shaped roof. Before reaching the temple, we walked by a giant mound surrounded by prayer flags and passed two women in different states of devotion: one in a faded red tunic who slowly circumambulated while turning her clicking wooden prayer wheel and moving her mouth, and the other in dark blue prostrating in silence, her small gray head gently touching the dusty ground again and again.

Everyone who practiced here at Drakarpo had to hike up the long steep road to the monastery that foreign visitors are allowed to drive up, their mouths moving as they murmured mantras and fingered their beads. I was beginning to figure out something about work and dedication here, something similar to the unfolding of daily life in Burma and Cambodia—an inexorable interconnection of life and faith (devotion). The lives of these two women seemed to be shaped by a deep love of practice, and as I watched them, I hungered for their devotion. Then the relentless score-keeping voice in my head began (again) to note my various inconsistent Buddhist habits, the absence of a deep conviction, and periodic avoidance of hard work. I felt sad about that and about my Western culture that seemed to lack this depth of commitment to loving-kindness.

In the Bhutan that I visited, most monasteries were built on high ground, far from the distractions of daily life in the lowland villages, and it required huge concentrated effort for the locals to travel there by foot. The country we traversed was dotted with small groups of pilgrims who walked hundreds of miles over treacherous ground to arrive at the monastery of their teacher, or to show up for a cremation ceremony and family gathering. "Right effort." This was one of the Buddha's core teachings from the Eightfold Path that frees us from suffering, and I was surrounded by it, understanding it for perhaps the first time.

Life is uncertain, death can come at any time, the Buddha taught a very long time ago, and so *constancy* in every moment was needed. And don't forget *karma*. For all your actions, there will be results. And so on through the generations. And what about reincarnation? I had always wanted to believe in the possibility of an ever-changing continuum with many more opportunities to attain peace and wisdom. But even though it often seems to me that I've known and inhabited a number of unfamiliar places in the far-off distant past, such as churches or monasteries, I find it hard to believe in a multitude of other lives beyond this one. From some of our thoughtful conversations about Bhutanese beliefs, I saw that there was no doubt in Karma's mind that he expected to move through many more lives before he was freed from ignorance and attachment; convinced that the path to enlightenment was long indeed, he took the coming back again and again for granted. As I listened to him, I yearned for the clarity and poise that anchored him in his beliefs.

The Drakarpo monastery was small and humble inside, with very worn dark wooden floors and walls covered with complicated, wildly colorful scroll paintings depicting different Buddhas and demon gods, and an altar to Padmasambhava with smoldering candles and bowls of fruit, where we made an offering of incense. I watched Karma prostrate himself on a well-worn part of the old wooden floor, a smooth caved-in spot where heads had been bowing for centuries. I wanted to bow, to feel what it was like to "let go" of thoughts and plans, but I felt awkward and shy, so I touched my hand to my heart. The head monk told us this was a "blessed" place where only those with the "right karma" could come. Strangely he made sense to me, and I didn't ask about it further. Just trust what comes your way.

More than ten years earlier, in the bustling Mahamuni marketplace in Mandalay, I'd learned about trust from a no-nonsense Burmese merchant. This man responded to my incessant queries about the authenticity of a particular antique lacquer begging bowl I was interested in by saying with a deep sigh, "This bowl you wish to buy is indeed quite old, Madam. Please trust me. You must remember that Buddhists never lie." Perhaps I already knew this, but how did I know? Moments later I left the little crowded stall with my beautiful old black lacquer monk's bowl carefully wrapped in newspaper and tied meticulously with twine. This man's words that urged me to trust stayed with me, and ultimately helped me find compassion for a little girl who had grown up in a world of half-truths, confusion, and many dark losses; a place where I had trouble holding on to or believing in truth, because the ground I'd traveled on was so very shaky and uncertain.

Discovering My Father's Truth, San Francisco—1958

In the summer of 1958, I returned home from Europe to visit my family, filled with memories of my last year and my new-found love for my Sicilian beau, Concetto. My bubble-like optimism and grand plans for the summer were shattered that June afternoon when my father came up the stairs of my grandmother's house and burst into tears.

Earlier that day I'd said goodbye to my mother, who was staying in New York with family, and boarded a plane for San Francisco. I was both nervous and excited to see my father after more than five years in which he had essentially vanished from my life. I hoped to begin to get to know him again, spending time at his big house on Filbert Street and maybe discovering a new family with him. He and Carol had just adopted a baby girl, and I was eager to meet this new little being. When my New York plane arrived at San Francisco International, I was expecting to see him waiting for me, but instead saw my grandparents standing there poised and deadly serious. I threw myself at Grandmother instinctively and cast a casual "hi" to my grandfather. She told me my father couldn't be there because just hours before his baby girl of three months had choked to death after being offered a grape by the child of a friend. An innocent child's attempt at generosity had proved fatal. I wouldn't be going to stay at his house after all, as planned, because my stepmother Carol was distraught and out of her mind with shame and grief.

Now I stood at the top of the grand stairs in my grandmother's house, waiting for my father to arrive. I was impatient and worried about what to say. I heard the key in the door and saw him plod upward, his beautiful white head cast down. Despite his luminous thick white hair with the tight curls, my father had never looked old to me. He was holding on to the railing as he came, moving as though in a dream. It took a while for him to reach the top. It seemed that we were all in slow motion. I stared at the dark formal painting of a Gadsden ancestor just over the stairs, waiting for words to come, and all that I was aware of then was the sugary perfume of her beloved cook Daily's fresh-baked butter cookies coming from the kitchen. Grandmother waited right beside me, placing her hand on my shoulder as though to steady herself. It was so still . . .o just the smell of her lavender hand lotion, the sounds of her soft breathing, and my father's silent slow steps on the dark carpeted stairs.

"Oh, Mother, oh, Mother," he moaned over and over, trying to hold himself together. "Oh, Mag, dear, you're here at last!" I saw a line of tears fall from his clear blue eyes, and I didn't know what to do. There he was, crying right there in front of me. I had never seen him cry. His little baby girl, Polly, had just died today, and he came now to Grandmother's house for comfort, an escape from the horror of his own empty home and a woman driven mad moving from room to room. He looked so tired.

I threw myself at him, wrapping my short arms around his skinny chest, feeling its solidity. "Oh, Daddy, I'm so sad. How terrible!" I had never seen a grown man cry before— maybe I assumed men just didn't do that, I don't know—come to think of it, I had never seen my father show anything that resembled emotion back in the days when we had been a little family together. Whatever grief he carried all those years as my mother turned away from him, he had buried deep inside, and soon he became someone who didn't feel. Or at least that's what it had looked like to me.

I tried to squeeze him harder, moving in closer now. "I don't know what to say," I muttered. "I love you, Daddy!" He just stood there stiffly at the top of the stairs, looking lost, held in the urgent embrace of the fourteen-year-old daughter he barely knew. And it seemed that the long five years that had passed since we had last seen each other dissolved into this moment, and we just stayed close to one another, together finally.

I tried to conjure images of his little Polly in my mind, newly arrived all pink and squirming in her new home, so I could see something tangible in the midst of this scary story, and at the same time I felt inside a cold dread, the horror at something as unnatural as a baby's death. I think my father had so wanted to fill the hole of childlessness in his life when he remarried; he wanted to create a whole new family so he could feel complete, and because they couldn't have any of their own, he and Carol decided to adopt this precious little being. It had taken a long time, I'm told, to find her. And now she was being shipped off to a mortuary to be put in a miniature casket.

I felt his body soften as we stood there, pressed together at the top of Grandmother's stairs. I felt the dampness of his chest and began to cry myself. All of a sudden, I was a little girl again with my father right here before me, and his heart was opening, I could feel it; I felt proud I was his daughter. We really saw each other, and I felt useful. Would he and I ever find a way back to each other through this terrible loss?

But why did this random thought come now in the midst of all this grief? I was sure I had lost him years before when he wandered away from my mother and me, defeated and rejected, turning his face away from me because I reminded him of my mother. But in this frightful moment, he had lost his little Polly, and his wife was on the edge of madness, and he needed me. That was all that was true. Loss hung everywhere around us under Grandmother's gaze as she gently led us into the living room for coffee and cookies.

May we practice in our lives for the benefit of all beings

In the courtyard of Paro's Kichyu monastery, which is the oldest in the country, stands a cheerful and perky orange tree that, according to locals, always produces fruit no matter what the season. On this November afternoon, the tree was loaded with plump miniature oranges. An old man in a dirty gray tunic dozed as he leaned up against the outside of the building in the afternoon sun, his whiskers bristling in the bright light, and a dusty black dog by his side. We passed him by to enter the sanctuary where a small group of younger monks were performing a chanting ceremony for a local person who had recently died, their golden robes lighting up the dark interior.

I slowly lowered myself to sit on the dark wooden floor and strained my eyes to see the painted gold-and-red Tibetan figures in the dim light; pungent incense smoke hung in the air and made me sleepy. Between me and the monks, I saw another one of those beautiful dips in the dark floor wood, this one a pear-shaped bowl where the devout had prostrated and prayed for more years than we'd ever know. It seemed to be the perfect shape for a small sleeping child, I thought. Somewhere in this holiest of holies were some rare relics from Padmasambhava, but it apparently wasn't the right time to be able to view them. I returned three times during my stay to this cozy little monastery where I felt at home, all the time trying to understand what it was about these sacred places that felt so very familiar. I found an old indefinable comfort here. Was it time now to reexamine my ideas about reincarnation and consider whether I had once lived life as a renunciate?

Above the monastery, I noticed a cremation ground swept clean of ashes from the last ceremony. Karma told me that people who held significant positions in the Paro community were invited to hold their cremation ritual here, and I remember thinking that sounded odd; how could it be that there was a class system in this gentle, highly democratic culture? After my recent visit to India, with its sprawling landscape colored by the caste system, I had found Bhutan's small society by contrast egalitarian and comforting. And much more peaceful. Perhaps it was the absence of garbage and plastic bags everywhere you traveled, and instead all those quaint little bright green cans nailed on posts throughout the countryside that proclaimed: "Use Me—Keep Bhutan Clean"; or the lack of palaces, sparkling silks and bangles, and aggressive beggars that suggested a very different universe; or perhaps just my fervent wish that it be so. It seemed that in this country, the spiritual practice stretched to include the environment.

Keeping a Promise in San Francisco—1958

When I was fourteen years old and in love, I made the momentous and unexpected choice to be baptized. I had just returned from Italy, where I had been living, to spend the summer with family, and I had decided to enter a church and be anointed by a minister all because my newfound Sicilian boyfriend,

Concetto, was terrified I would go to hell otherwise. Our improbable romance was awash in cultural disconnects and our age difference was six years, but neither of us could see that in the summer of '58. He was Catholic like the majority of children in Italy, and like most Catholics believed that baptism was a necessary choice if you wished to avoid hell and damnation. Up to now I had been a proud athcist, conditioned by my left-leaning family, but this summer I had listened to him speak about the nuns in school, the Virgin Mary and God, and taking confession, and his words pulled me in closer. I'm sure I wasn't able then to understand the depth of his beliefs, but part of me just wanted to join him where he was.

I was looking for a portion of safety and thought I knew the way. This baptism choice became a gift to my grandmother Lavinia as well; she had helped raise me and, through the years, quietly regretted my rejection of the spiritual. Her religion had always been a personal one, and she had never once suggested I read the Bible, go to church, or even believe in God. Perhaps she'd trusted that I would eventually find my way. I was named for her, she had nurtured me, and I adored her with all my heart.

When I told her over lunch one day after I returned home that I wanted to be baptized, I was happy to see her so gratified at this odd change in my ways. She was visibly pleased and asked few questions. It was enough for her that I was finally making a wise choice. She arranged the ceremony at an old Protestant church in her neighborhood, and soon I found myself standing before the white marble font with her by my side, both of us in proper and sober suits and white gloves. Bowing my head, I mumbled the words of agreement and trust, and felt the cold sprinkle of the water on my forehead. I never questioned the minister's somber words, nor did I ever admit to her that I had been driven by the love and superstition of my young Sicilian. It just seemed easier that way at the time, and I always assumed I would find the time to explain it all to her when I was older and braver. Sadly, this never happened.

I finally discovered that spiritual refuge she had wished for me, although it was many years later and through means she might not have expected. In 1995, in the mountains of northern New Mexico, I discovered a small Insight Meditation community and the possibility of coping with my ancient dark suffering. It saddened me that, by the time I discovered the Buddha's teachings in the late 1990s, my grandmother had let go of living and was on to her new "adventure" in the afterlife. With her huge inquisitive mind, she would have loved talking about the Buddha, I knew it; in her own unique way she had led the life of a Buddha, despite being raised in the lap of privilege in a stratified white America. Her own Buddha qualities came through in her various moments of wisdom, generosity, love, and fairness. She had always wanted safety and happiness for me, and I knew she would have been glad that the path I had symbolically embraced at fourteen in San Francisco had ultimately flourished. It was no surprise that the remote high mountains of Bhutan reminded me of the rugged and mysterious New Mexico landscape where my spiritual journey began.

Finding My Path in Taos, New Mexico—1995

It was a beautiful autumn afternoon in northern New Mexico, and my new friend and massage therapist, Diane, was working on my body as a crisp chill blew in through the open windows. She used several heated gray stones, moving them up and down my small back, as I inhaled the cedar incense she had burning and felt ease seep into my bones. I loved this new relationship with the dark-haired woman with the large hands, a place where I didn't have to speak or be clever to be connected. Softly, she said, "You are holding a lot of grief in your body . . . so much suffering." White cotton curtains moved with the afternoon breeze and her cozy studio felt like a cocoon as I thought to myself, *Yes, more years than I can count.* She touched me with warm hands, strong and gentle all at once, and I could feel her breath touching the back of my neck, and I allowed it all to enter my tired forty-something body that felt leaden and neglected and ached with undefined hunger.

All the psychotherapy I had done in my life so far had not cracked the mystery or opened the door to self-love. The more I talked to therapists—from the time I was eight and pulling out my beautiful curly hair strand by strand, to the time in my thirties when I boasted to my therapist that I finally had told my mother she was a failure—the more I noticed that I had been looking always to others for love: a mother who didn't know how, a young husband who resisted me and our marriage, and finally an emotionally crippled partner whom I thought I could change. There had been others along the way, mainly young men who showed up during my marriage and offered some quick intimacy, only to evaporate from my life because of wrong place, wrong time, wrong person, wrong conditions. I was dog-tired, I could feel that now, and I was sick of blaming others for my pain, no matter how righteous it felt at the time. I was exhausted from not knowing who I was and how I felt and pretending that I did. "You're right, Diane. I am worn out from all this sadness inside. I don't know what to do anymore. I was thinking it would be good to meditate, but I don't think I'm cut out for it somehow."

I rested now in her studio, filled with reminders of

another kind of life that followed the Buddha's way of kindness and compassion: a beautiful small carved statue of the goddess Quan Yin on the altar, worn dark wooden *mala* beads, bold Japanese calligraphy hanging from the walls, and always a stick of peppery sandalwood incense before a photograph of her beloved Zen master Kobin. As she moved the hot stones across my back, my body slowly found some rest. "It's not complicated, you know . . ." she had said when I asked her about how to meditate, "it's just a breath-by-breath, a moment-by-moment thing, being with what comes, accepting yourself and others, no judgment, but compassion . . . and seeing how everything changes. Take a little in breath now, see how it feels, Mag." Into my knotted-up body and mind, so certain that meditation meant only renunciation and lonely gray suffering, her words landed and took form. Her sunny trusting face with its rosebud smile and full cheeks, those strong hands, warm body, and deep wisdom, brought me into myself that afternoon; it felt a little like what I imagined home was. Within a few weeks, I walked into my very first meditation group and never looked back.

May all beings realize their true nature

On my last day in Paro, I returned to Kichyu monastery and was invited to be a guest at the cremation ceremony of a local village woman. Earlier in our time together, I had told Karma of my interest in death and dying and my many years of hospice work, and that afternoon he arranged for the two of us to be silent participants at the gathering. The ritual was seamlessly orchestrated, and it began with the arrival of a retinue of monks who proceeded to play their giant long horns as others clanged many different brass bells, and everyone waited for the resident lama to come. He arrived after a long lull of anticipation and began to chant the necessary prayers for the deceased woman. A simple altar—a long table with shiny yellow and red oilcloth—was set up with soda bottles, some tin vessels for offerings, and a small bowl of fruit. The pyre was a plain structure of large stones set in a square form with wood carefully placed on top to create a small, slightly pointed mound, making me think of the whimsical pointed roofs that I had seen everywhere. The woman's body was encased in this structure, and thus barely visible.

After sprinkling water and some mysterious white powder onto the nearby wood, and chanting of more prayers, one monk in red-and-gold robes ignited the pyre with a small smoldering stick. As the white powder hit the blaze, a beautiful show of brilliant sparks shot up into the air. The afternoon light softened to golden, and the family members, primarily men in plain blue tunics, came one by one to tend the wood on the fire, then returned to their places on the ground where food was arranged in a number of plastic containers. Karma and I observed from a spot above everyone, sitting on a couple of logs, and it looked to me that, as they talked quietly to one another, they were just having a family picnic. All I remember hearing was the crackling of burning wood, and some birds calling from a distant tree. The pyre burned very slowly, and I struggled to conjure this invisible woman, her life, and her dreams.

Karma walked with me to one side of the mound so I could view a part of the body now that the wood had burned down some. I moved cautiously, not wanting to be obvious, then I saw sizzling flesh and oozing bubbling fluid amid the purple smoke; her tiny rib cage appeared through the flames all stark and sculptural. She had been tied up in a seated posture as is their tradition. Smoke was thick above the flames, swirling up and away into a stridently blue sky. Invigorated by the perfume of burning wood, I watched carefully. As I moved around, I began to see her small skull, smoothly round, standing out among the angular burned logs. The sight of this brilliantly white whole skull gave me a start, so solid was it among the disintegrating parts of her little body. I backed away to take it all in.

One of the fire tenders then took a long branch and tapped hard on the skull; there was a thunk, and it cracked open. A small part fell away, and brain matter spilled to the ground, a slippery mass of yellow and pink. The skull continued to burn slowly, and as parts of it fell away, the face of the woman appeared, changing subtly as the fire burned and danced, the eye sockets, nose, and mouth now darkly visible.

"It looks like she's smiling," Karma whispered to me. I didn't see the smile, but instead just a moment-by-moment shifting of what had once been a human face.

"It's beautiful," I replied. Yes, the whole show was beautiful: the mass of swirling blue, yellow, and gray flame, and her tiny fragment of a face dancing there, coming in and out of focus. After first recoiling when her head was struck, I settled into watching the ephemeral melting away of her countenance; I remember thinking it was taking a long time to disappear, and this seemed somehow fitting. The work of coming into life and then departing from it may be life's greatest mystery, and a body on fire takes its own time to dissolve into dust. From time to time I caught a rank odor, like the burning of rotten meat, greasy and sour, and then it floated away, as once again I inhaled the dreamy burning wood smoke.

It had been at least four hours since we had settled into this ritual, and I was reluctant to go. The sun disappeared, and cold was starting to sweep through the valley as I began to think about the long journey that lay ahead of me, the crossing of many time zones to arrive home in California. I made an offering at their altar before leaving and was given a small gift of money and a deep bow by one of the family members, a kindness that made me a little weepy. An unknown visitor in their land from far away, I bowed in gratitude for the invitation to be a witness.

To put the dead body on the mountaintop as the Tibetans do, or burn the body on the pyre and allow the transformation to occur makes sense to me. In America, we embalm people and put them in caskets or have them cremated in ovens, not in the open air; we rarely make a ritual of the burning. We lack reverent ceremony in the West, I believe, because we have an uncomfortable and fearful relationship with death. We have funerals in churches, wakes in the home, we tell stories, dress in black, try to control our tears, and load grief on our backs for all the years to come. Since the age of eight or nine, I have followed a "less traveled" path, and for the last fifteen years I have been drawn to dying, both caring for the mortally ill and being part of the ceremony surrounding death that Buddhist tradition offers. I want what feels real and touchable—the colors, the body, the smells, the flames, the chanting, the prayers, the ashes, and then the deep and lasting emptiness. And the grief that stretches out beyond what we can see, as palpable as the body and the flames and the songs.

Twenty-five years ago, my grandmother, who had always wanted me to find the solace of a spiritual path, died peacefully at the age of eighty-nine, allowing her body to waste away in the hospital following a traumatic burn accident. She announced her plans to family members as we gathered in her hospital room, she apologized for any sadness and suffering that would come to us, and she went calmly and naturally, having abstained from food and water for well over a week. I sat and watched all the small physical changes, the shriveling and shrinking of her body and the stilling of her voice, the declining of the breath . . . and I spoke to her softly as she went. I bore witness in the peaceful, very white and sterile hospital room, as she showed me her way, curled gracefully into a fetal shape underneath the crisp white sheets, her body engaged in its final work.

The sight of the fiercely burning fire at Kiychu monastery that afternoon in Paro and the dissolving face and skull of the unnamed woman gave me the same comfort I had experienced at the bedside of my grandmother as she let go before my eyes and left me behind. Though I'd probably felt in that moment that she had disappeared forever from my life, I came to see it differently in the years that followed. There may be no real disappearing, either in Children's Hospital or in Paro, Bhutan, but instead a mysterious indefinable transformation of life's energy as the human soul leaves the body. Ashes to ashes, and blessings to you both . . . and may we all go so quietly and gently, and beautifully, into that dark night.

Six: Duality and
Impermanence in India

We clambered out of our bus on a dusty hot afternoon
in Udaipur to look for our guide's favorite spice store,
so that a handful of us could scoop up some special local
pepper, turmeric, and even some saffron to add to the piles
of silks and shiny baubles we had already purchased. That
grumpy, unsocial part of myself that hated following orders
and being forced to be social reminded me of how I disliked
being herded about with others, all this unfolding quietly
inside as Ramesh took a martial stance and barked his directions for us to cross the wide street. Despite my reputation for
taking on adventures alone, I had capitulated to group travel
so I could have a safe, stress-free, first-time experience of
India. We were an oddly assorted bunch on this Metropolitan
Museum "grand tour" of north and south India: a number of
East Coast retired couples with plenty of shopping money
and expensive leisure clothes; a single tall bookish woman
from Washington, DC, who showed little or no interest in
Indian culture; the requisite dowagers whose little reading
glasses hung down on pretty silk cords; well-traveled widows

with facelifts and fragile personas; and me, a "wild card" from the West on my first journey into the beautiful chaos of India, hungry to learn all I could about its history and religion. I asked our trip leader nagging questions about the Hindu gods, the wandering cows, and the British Raj, while a number of the other women on the bus talked about how soon they might get a manicure or find a good deal on sari material.

Today, our handsome Rajasthani guide, Ramesh, showed great equanimity as he shepherded our vocal (and primarily female) group across a road that teemed with wildly colorful honking buses and loaded-down bicycles weaving every which way to the small storefront with cracked yellow paint, red signage, and dirty windows. A handful of us squeezed through a narrow door, slowly adjusting our eyes to the dark, while a bitter and earthy spiced perfume greeted us. Burlap bags lay everywhere. There were hundreds of dusty jars on shelves with indecipherable writing, and of course small containers of all kinds containing the coveted Indian spices in ochre and brown. My nose twitched and burned, and I wanted to sneeze from all the pepper in the air; I felt breathless from the claustrophobic space and decided to hurry along with the shopping and get out into the daylight.

A woman with a model's figure and cool composure waited outside—her name was Michelle Drummond. She was a well-dressed young Frenchwoman, married to a successful New York lawyer, who had been holding his Blackberry to his ear much of the time as we marched through the series of ancient temple sites in Madurai and Chennai in the south; he couldn't (wouldn't) travel without his phone for business, she said, and that was that. The two had shared some stories over dinner of exotic-sounding places like Dubai and Abu Dabi that they had visited together for business and pleasure, but their tales betrayed little cultural curiosity. I watched her nervousness now in the dusty street as a few grimy-faced little children stared up at her expectantly, and then moved in closer. Their clothes hung unevenly on their tiny bodies as their skinny arms and hands flailed every which way, making escape impossible. In crisp white linen, she looked out of place, too clean, too bright, and too white—but mostly too clean. Her long red glossy manicured nails invited extra attention.

The small beggars beseeched her for money and came in even closer, calling out, "Lady, we're hungry . . . lady, something for our baby sister here . . . lady, gimme some, gimme some money. . . ."

She called out to our dignified and patient American guide who waited at the store's entrance, "Get them away from me! . . . They're so *dirty*!" One arm rose up as if to cover her lovely face that looked pinched and repulsed; I wanted to turn away from her distress, but instead I kept watching as her panic slowly fizzled into stony silence, the children still swarming, and Olivier not attending to her. I'm not sure if any of my fellow travelers saw this quick scene unfold, and I can't remember how she extricated herself from the army of beggars, but before long it had dissipated like a small fragment of the day's noisy unfolding, except in my mind.

Where was the compassion? So far on this journey, the chaos and pathos of India—its dusty, dirty temples and marketplaces, wild street children, and scrawny cows looking for food—had been slowly cracking open my heart, and I'd begun to think of human deprivation in a way I never had before. Mrs. Drummond's revulsion made me uncomfortable and confused. I wanted to assume that she had just as much good will and generosity in her heart as the next person—it is inherent in most humans, after all—but her panic at what was alien seemed to keep compassion at bay. We all have this fear, which is part of meeting the challenging experiences as we travel into an unknown future; and it seems also that we have the capacity to see foreignness for what it is and let it work its own magic, become less foreign, and pass on through. It mattered not that she had traveled the globe with her successful husband and seen countless dark-skinned people in different cultures; she had probably traveled everywhere first class and been cushioned from desperation. In the end, few people heard her that day, and I imagine she tucked the whole thing away in the "challenging travel experience" file in her mind as she sipped her pre-dinner glass of chardonnay. Did Mrs. Drummond's ostensible indifference have this weight for me, I wonder, because of all the times I'd passed by a homeless person on San Francisco streets with my face averted, or when I chose to buy a box seat at the opera instead of giving money to Meals on Wheels? Did hypocrisy play a part in my indignation?

Travelers to India are usually told about the great numbers of children who are organized into syndicates, networks run behind the scenes, usually by well-to-do men who drive them to hit the streets every day and beg with all their might. These young people receive little of what they pry out of tourists' guilty white hands, and they remain filthy, underdressed, hungry, and unsupported. First-time visitors are warned to avoid contact with these sad children, asked to still their bleeding hearts and remember that giving money to them is like handing money to a desperate prostitute under the thumb of some greedy kingpin. These children are skilled at swarming and surrounding the wide-eyed visitors, expanding in numbers as they look up with coal black eyes and hair like weeds, pleading for attention. Saying no doesn't often work very well, for they've perfected the art of persistent harassment, ever-present in all the alleys with cracked sidewalks, finally thrusting in your face a sickly little baby to further deepen the guilt.

These young beggars lead invisible lives off the streets, disappearing at night into the sprawling slums and keeping watch as their family members and friends sicken and die in rickety cardboard huts that smell of human waste and rotting garbage. Many have siblings who work at garbage collecting to make money, as their fathers fall into inebriated despair at home and their mothers work against all odds to steer a course through the misery: cooking, cleaning, and sewing, and carrying the most helpless ones on their hips. The lives of the untouchables are unimaginable to most of us who have never lived in India, as is the mind state of the raving men in the countryside who gang-rape young girls who venture out into the fields to relieve themselves. The numbers of young women who are attacked and killed has seized public attention in the media in the last few years, and I fear the subjugation continues as India's judicial system, controlled primarily by men, has shown little skill in finding justice.

The fabric of Indian society appears tragically torn. I was struck by the uneasy marriage of this country's deep spiritual traditions and the inhumanity visited on women for reasons I could hardly fathom: poverty, despair, and the consequences of overpopulation. As I traveled, I tried to visualize the unfolding of the Buddha's teachings here in India, the imparting of wisdom and love as he walked the countryside until he was finally too old to carry on. It felt to me as though this landscape should still be imbued with his compassion and wisdom, but what we were bombarded with in the winter of 2008 were the Hindu devotional practices swirling and unfolding around the clock in the villages, spilling out into the streets and alleys with music and sticky sweet incense, waves of body odor and giant smiles, all of it driven by a passion to have a perfect union with the gods—not the Buddha. And the question of violence against the feminine remains unanswered, at least at this point in my relationship to India. All I could conclude was that the spiritual backbone of India comes inexplicably hand in hand with mundane, unspiritual, and violent acts.

Most of the four weeks I traveled through India, I attempted to be a witness to these desperate children—to look them in the face, squarely, while at the same time resisting their pleas and maintaining my boundaries. No easy feat. We are not used to this in the West, in particular the witnessing. I was now traveling alone for the first time, separated from my partner after a long and unfulfilling relationship, and I had no cushion against the waves of chaotic desire, no companion to steer me away from all the chaos, or distract me with suggestions for our next meal or textile shop. For about fourteen years, I had traveled to many far-flung places with a man who loved to run interference and take charge of whatever was needed. He was a painter who had great charm and much knowledge about culture, and he was also a control freak. But now I stood alone looking into these sad faces, haunted by what I didn't know.

When we returned day after day from the long hot hours of touring to the Oberoi Hotel, a palatial abode with celadon-colored silk curtains and marble floors, bejeweled mirrors and turbaned attendants, I often felt giddy, unsteady on my feet, pausing to sniff the fat bouquets of damp pink roses in crystal bowls. Is it possible to be immune to having our hearts and determination tested? There would be no wild little children to darken these regal hallways this evening. And yet . . . they continued to darken my mind, reminding me of the heartbreaking boundaries in life. Navigating this disturbing dichotomy in India felt like being on some hallucinogenic drug trip in some ways, the dusty dirty noisy gritty world of the poor bleeding unpredictably into the palaces guarded by colorfully decorated camels with long eyelashes that bowed to you when you arrived. I knew there must be a different Indian landscape beyond this experience, where the duality might not be so disturbing, and I realized I wasn't able or ready to see it yet.

The Indians might say to you that the child beggars are simply playing their designated part in the caste system, the entrenched segregation that has evolved over centuries to manage the problem of the enormous diversity of beings arriving here to find their home, and that these castes are in fact a means to make an out-of-control population more orderly. Where we from the West find jarring contradictions in this chaotic and cruel society and rush to judgment, they see things manifesting *just as they are*. Not bad not good, just this way.

Back at my fancy hotel after the sensory onslaught of our spice shopping, I slowed down to look down at my hands in front of a sparkling bright mirror, little fists all clean and white and plump. And I recalled the snot-covered brown fingers and cheeks of those little worker bees in the system that rushed relentlessly toward me every day—in front of temples, markets, shops, spice stores, and hotels—to crush my heart in each moment. The sparkling environment I had just entered created only a temporary refuge, I knew this. This phantasmagoria of sensations I moved through felt just as unreal as the swirling landscape of the deprived right outside the gates, and even cocktails and a good night's sleep couldn't erase my sadness as I tried to navigate this confusing dualistic world.

When I went to graduate school in my forties, I found some intellectual heroes who ultimately became lifelong companions. Anna Karenina, one of Tolstoy's most realized female characters, was such a hero. She was an upper-class Russian woman who, because she followed her heart instead of society's rules, became an "untouchable" in her patriarchal nineteenth-century world. I believe Tolstoy's compassion for women made it possible for him to create this fully tragic female character who appeared to have everything necessary for a successful life until she sought her own happiness. He begins the novel with these words: "Happy families are all alike; every unhappy family is unhappy in its own way," and the trajectory of the narrative becomes clear.

Because Anna falls in love with a man outside her marriage and will not give him up, she falls from grace, is ostracized from society and ultimately driven to despair and madness. Lonely in her marriage to her husband Karenin, she tries hopelessly to resist the affections of the handsome Count Vronksy, but in the end her hunger for love is too strong, and she succumbs. Although men during this period in history generally had freedom in their personal relations, women were required to remain cushioned in prescribed roles, no matter what was buried inside. Tolstoy's heroine couldn't do this and soon became a pariah. Deranged and desperate, she throws herself under a train when she sees there was no escape for her in her exile and suffering. In the end, both India's caste structure and Tolstoy's portrait of nineteenth-century Russia remind me that alienation from those we hold dear is a dark, and often inevitable human tragedy.

Some Untouchables in My Past

Being a Stranger in Florida—1963

I was "a stranger in a strange land" in Winter Park, Florida, on a November afternoon in 1963. A bunch of us crammed into David's pale blue Cadillac convertible and headed off for the beach with cases of Budweiser stashed in the trunk. On our way, we stopped at a lonely gas station around noon so someone could buy cigarettes. I happened to be here in the land of palm trees because I had been expelled from my first-choice college in Ohio for living off-campus with my boyfriend, Jack. My mother's brother, who was used to managing things, quickly came up with the idea of Rollins College when my mother made it clear she didn't want me living in her New York apartment for the coming year. In September of 1963, I boarded a train, dressed in a dark red suit with a fur collar and a strand of real pearls that had been handed down to me, and I promised myself I'd just put my head down and work hard to get good grades for a year so I could return to Antioch and my beloved young beau.

Many of my cohorts were at Rollins because they came from rich families who needed a convenient place to park their kids for the full four years while they sorted themselves out. I saw quickly that this was not a serious institution of higher learning, and that most of my companions seem to have little or no thought of making their way in the world. Dex and Ruthie and Bob, David, Sonny, and . . . who else was headed to the beach that day? I can't remember—fo it was quite a blurry time, to say the least; too much beer and too many late nights. I also figured out I could probably drink my way through this college chapter, trusting that my not-so-admirable balancing act of closet drinking and serious study that had worked in high school would work here as well. I tagged along with this unlikely group of wealthy misfits who talked about rock n' roll and booze, and not about writers or scientists or social change; many of them felt entitled and complained regularly about their parents and all they weren't doing for them.

I was mildly attracted to this fellow named Dexter, a very white guy from Chicago who played great rock 'n' roll piano and tried to channel Jerry Lee Lewis. He had ash blond hair, a squared off jaw, and chilly blue eyes. I wasn't crazy about his elitist way of talking, but when I kept up with the rum and Cokes at the drive-in, I noticed it bothered me less and less. I lived in a dorm with other girls who had chosen not to join sororities, and we spent a lot of our time either playing bridge or planning midnight outings with different guys. Forever the responsible student, however, I forced myself to go to all my classes and do the work, and I managed to accomplish all this while spending a lot of time with the party crowd.

We coasted into the gas station, beer already on ice in the trunk, and Bob hopped out to buy some cigarettes. I noticed a large group of customers huddled inside the mini mart, staring at something we couldn't see. On my way to the bathroom, I paused on the fringe of the crowd, and eventually picked up some sounds from a little television set playing in the cashier's office. The next thing I remember was hearing Walter Cronkite making this sober announcement as his normally composed face quivered with emotion: "Today at Parkland Hospital in Dallas, Texas, at precisely 1:00 p.m., the president of the United States, John F. Kennedy, was pronounced dead from a gunshot wound to the brain." The various customers just stood there. Frozen in time. I grappled for meaning inside my head—this country's smart young president assassinated in Dallas, Texas, a landscape that had never been friendly to him, the man from an aristocratic Catholic family who had swept the voting public off their feet with his eloquent vision and seemed poised at the beginning of a brilliant political life. Young John Fitzgerald Kennedy was now dead. It had been just a couple of years ago, hadn't it, that my mother and I had stayed up all night watching election returns as Kennedy pulled out a tense victory against the dark and awkward Richard Nixon, and she was so happy she wanted to dance in the hallway at eight in the morning. The United States had finally elected a liberal educated man who spoke of politics like a poet.

I returned to the car and my beach-going pals and exclaimed, "President Kennedy is dead . . . how awful. I can't believe it!"

And my piano-playing friend said, "Good riddance! He wasn't any good . . . a damn Catholic!" I looked at him and my companions, and everything around me seemed to shift and vibrate; I was now (or had I always been?) in a very separate universe. It almost felt like vertigo. I looked around as cars came in and went out, people bought their candy and cigarettes, and I felt a deadly queasiness. The country's president had been murdered, and in this gas station in Winter Park, Florida, very few reacted. No tears. No sadness. Just the smell of gasoline, popcorn, and car exhaust. I piled into the back of the light blue convertible with all the others as my disorientation started to fade, and someone said, "Oh, Mag, pretty soon, you won't even care—we're going to have a blast today! He wasn't right for this country . . . way too liberal. . . ." Then Dave hit the accelerator, I put on my sunglasses and soon felt warmth and wind on my face. That alone felt real. I was clearly an alien of sorts; I didn't belong here. Then my mind went blank in self-defense, I suspect, as I looked ahead to an afternoon of drinking and whatever amnesia that might bring.

My Mother and the Bum—San Francisco and Taos—Seventies Onward

One winter afternoon in Taos, New Mexico, where I had retreated in my mid-forties to escape my broken marriage, I stopped for gas at the Chevron station on the main road into town. It was bitter cold that December in 1992, and the fog hung thick over the mountains, with moisture in the air that hinted at a possible snowfall. It felt bone-chilling, this high mountain winter cold. As I began to pump my gas, I saw a lone male figure wrapped in a frayed gray blanket walking unsteadily alongside the mini mart, with a pint-sized paper bag clutched in one hand. His small figure off in the distance held my attention, and I wanted to see his face. I imagined that under that blanket he had dull tired eyes and a grizzled, dark brown countenance, not because he was Indian, but because many days of dirt and grime had not been wiped away. He wanted to disappear, become invisible, so he could drink his booze behind the gas station, unnoticed. He was probably used to hiding his shame. In that very moment, I saw my fifty-year-old mother dressed in her long blue muumuu wandering around the living room of her San Francisco apartment, making herself a scotch on the rocks, her dark red lipstick just recently applied. Having that first evening drink alone . . . she rather enjoyed that. She was about to join some guests in the living room after she found a light for her cigarette. She seemed always to be searching for that cigarette lighter somehow, and then the misplaced drink. Later that evening she would have a few more cocktails, and then a couple of large glasses of white wine at dinner as she absently pushed the food on her plate and smiled politely at her friends.

From the time I was pretty young, I had a habit of helping her in the kitchen—she always seemed to need it. And some decades back, most likely in the seventies, I began to find small juice glasses of vodka hidden in overhead cupboards or on shelves here and there. And each time I noticed these little forgotten glasses, my feelings became muddled and shaky. On the one hand, there was the familiarity of concealment—I knew this very well—I often hid shot glasses of straight gin in a secret compartment in my antique desk as I did my homework during the last two years of high school, showing an astonishing ability to balance mild inebriation with the memorizing of Shakespeare. And on the other hand, there was a deep sadness that came to me as I began to see how deeply addicted and alone she was, and how this was probably going to kill her.

Simply and inelegantly put, my mother was a drunk who lived in a fancy apartment and pretended otherwise. When she was a little girl growing up in Long Island in the twenties and thirties, people were never drunks, but instead they were people with "little drinking issues," and the cousins who committed suicide by swallowing arsenic just seemed to have died from unspecified causes. Though she usually dressed herself up pretty well, with costume jewelry and splashes of L'Heure Bleue perfume, she also had her personal pieces of shame: the ugly wide calloused feet she tried to squeeze into pretty flats, the gnarled hands that she didn't cherish anymore, and when I looked closely at her face, her lipstick always seemed cracked. As she grew older and gave herself less and less attention, I'd noticed food stains on her colorful dresses. If she carried shame, then so did I; we were partners in this shame—the embarrassment I felt for my own heaviness, crooked teeth, flat feet, and recurring melancholy and alienation—all this was just as dark and sad as my mother's untidiness. My mother's tucked-away secrets had always been part of our domestic landscape, but it was when I reached my forties and saw my marriage fraying at the edges that I first understood our common despair. This being "other" belonged to both of us. She tried to hide her dark addiction, and I tried to hide the hurt in my marriage by occasionally running away from my husband and kids. She eventually became yellow-skinned and bloated and paranoid with liver disease, and after twenty-five years of marriage, I finally rejected a decent but imperfect man who at one time had sworn that he wanted to grow old with me.

There were times over all those years when I was close to telling her that I knew what she was up to, but I never did. Conditioned by both my grandmother and my mother to act the right way and be "a good girl," I felt the weight of that every day and buried my anger. I had a deep reservoir of goodwill for my mother—it seems that children carry this kind of dedication no matter what, even when they are hunkered down in their beds at night hugging their stuffed toys and trying not to fall apart. I somehow let my righteousness go and allowed her to retain her dignity as the family matriarch.

I had worked so hard to be a kind person, but this next layer in our relationship felt like cowardice and fear. Like my passive silent father, I figured out that confronting this woman brought a great deal of chaos and suffering. Every once in a while, she took notice of my goodness and called me the perfect child as she gave me an expensive jade necklace from Saks Fifth Avenue or a quaint needlepoint pillow, but there was never a strong warm hug to go along with it. Good had always been the way of least resistance for me, and in this unstable relationship it was best not to resist. This unobtrusive kindness kept me from placing more judgment on her already broken heart. She was sliced in two, in a way: a gracious lady and a lost child who couldn't see who she really was, no different from the faceless Taos man whose defeated form had brought her to mind on that bitter winter afternoon. My mother and the lost man shared the shame of not being seen, of not seeing themselves in the world. My well-dressed traveling companion in India, Mrs. Drummond, believed as my mother always had in a carefully stratified world where people dined well, smoked filtered cigarettes, and felt separated from hardship. Neither my mother nor the lawyer's wife from New York could possibly have imagined that they were kindred beings with begging children in India or lonely bums in northern New Mexico.

Fred and His Cat on the Streets of San Francisco—1997

The young man I met on Market Street one fall afternoon stood by his shopping cart filled with a mix of indistinguishable belongings, accompanied by a small striped gray cat who sat on a well-worn little cushion close by, oblivious to the noisy stream of people marching past with appointments and jobs to go to. The year was 1997, and I was on my way to the passport office to renew travel documents. I paused to appreciate this innocent, oddly contented cat and began to talk to its owner, a small bright-faced young man in checkered red flannel shirt and dark blue baseball cap. I don't remember his name, so I'll call him Fred. He had been on the street for many months after moving out of a homeless shelter where his treasured family photograph album had been stolen from under his cot. He said homeless shelters were dangerous places. "You could end up dead there," he offered with a knowing grin, and on top of that they were no place for cats. I understood the loss of the photographs; as a girl, I had sat at my grandmother's side and watched intently and for many years as she turned the soft black pages covered with jagged-edged little snapshots with all the mysterious characters from her past; and when I grew up, I created many albums in order to hold on to the players in my family, and my adventures in foreign landscapes. It seems humans are compelled to construct books of memory in our lives, whether we live on the street or in a tidy suburban house, books that tell our stories and remind us we had a past, *life stories* where people appeared happy and normal at times, where there were grilled cheese sandwiches and days at the beach and someone to kiss us goodnight.

Fred reported his own story to me without self-pity. The theft was simply what happened in these crowded rooms, he said, where too many lonely and desperate people landed to get in out of the cold . . . places where transgressions happened for no particular reason other than providing a momentary distraction from misery and boredom. He went on to introduce me to his cat, Sally, certainly a good reason not to bed down in a shelter. I was happy he had this four-legged companion on his lonely journey; Sally the cat seemed to soften the hard edges for him. As people of all shapes and sizes marched by, we talked about politics, the city of San Francisco, and the great feeling of sunshine on your back on a chilly day, as we stood together in our small bubble, temporarily unseen by those around us. Eventually I realized it was time to move on, and I offered him a little cash as a gift, but he gracefully refused, sending me on my way. "I'm just grateful for the company, ma'am, just being seen, you know, and talking to someone who looks me in the eye," said he. I moved away reluctantly, looking back to catch another glimpse of this gentle man living in the moment with his little cat at her post by his shopping cart.

When I returned to the same place a week or so later, hoping to find Fred and Sally, they weren't there. No surprise. The world of street people changes moment by moment, day by day, and uncertainty is the rule. I thought a lot about him in the weeks to come and hoped that wherever he had parked his shopping cart, he and Sally were having a good conversation with someone who paused to pay attention.

"Attention must be paid," said Willy Loman's wife in *Death of a Salesman*, pleading for the compassion she felt was absent in her world. In her eyes all human beings, even her deluded, imperfect husband, were worthy of witnessing. In paying attention to one another, we discover our shared humanity. On Market Street that beautiful afternoon, Fred and Sally had reminded me of just that.

Impermanence on the River

A small group of us hustled through the busy narrow streets of Varanasi, making a beeline for the Great Mother River of India, and the boat that would carry us on our early morning journey. We were close to the end of the grand four-week trip, and by this time many of our contingent were weary both of one another and of early-morning activities that required focused attention. There were those too who were simply not very curious about this river that teemed with bathers, candles, and human waste. It was barely light, but the little streets we crossed hummed with activity: barber shops, vendors, tailors, dentists in their little outdoor offices, and of course the gentle brown cows meandering everywhere in front, around, and behind us. These Indian cows had an equanimous look on their faces as they joined the humans on the street, with frequent detours to consume more plastic and garbage. I came to love these Indian cows for their constancy and calm, happy that they seemed to be smiling in my direction; I worried about them too.

On one of our frequent seven-hour bus trips, one of my travel companions, a single dowager type from New York, commented from her window seat behind me that she thought it was wonderful that the cows were cleaning up so much of the street garbage. This followed her editorial remark about how disturbing it was that Indian society didn't do more to clean up the streets! Taken aback by her obvious lapse in understanding, I paused before saying a word. Did she not realize that the animals that eat large amounts of discarded plastic waste die from it? I asked myself. Of course not. Was it not important to point this out to her? Forgetting in that moment the unhappiness that comes from being reactive, I turned around and told her the story of a hungry African elephant whose intestines seized up and killed her after she devoured large numbers of plastic bags and bottles. Then I watched as her eyes glazed over with indifference and she looked away.

As night oozed slowly into morning, we all kept pretty quiet, carefully watching our footing and the cows in the murky light and trying to avoid the young human scavengers beginning their day. When I first saw the river, I remember feeling surprised it looked so ordinary and dirty, this body of water that all Indians considered so sacred, where they came by the thousands to anoint themselves again and again before they died. Stumbling across rocks and stones, we finally found our boatman, as some of our group tugged nervously at their jackets, pulling them closer and closer about their bodies. They seemed afraid: stories were dancing in their heads of squalid toxic waters that could make a Westerner sick as a dog. The waters of this river were blackish green, smelling of old clothes, animals, and garbage. Thick fog hung over the water, and we heard voices in sing-song rhythm and the rhythmic slapping of oars on the water; very little around us was visible. The sky began to get lighter, dark blue turning to misty pale gray as we were finally launched onto the river.

Water lapped against our boat and no one spoke. I breathed in slowly, waiting for the ritual to unfold. I saw small round votive candles floating in the grimy water, resembling little beacons bobbing around our boat. A small vessel moved slowly and silently alongside, completely equipped with trinkets, fabrics, postcards, incense, and beads—a floating souvenir shop! We pushed resolutely forward. Before too long, we could make out the ghats, the long flights of stone steps rising from the big river, and it seemed then as though a dusty antique painting had suddenly come alive as an epic congregation splashed joyously in the water, some fully dressed, others in very little at all. The women's saris shouted out with brilliant color—purples, reds, yellows, and blues, with so many sparkles—as they bent down to gather the murky water in their hands and splash themselves with much laughter. They washed clothes, their children, and themselves. I saw many men of different ages standing quietly, staring into space, their hands in namaste gesture, and children dunking themselves playfully in the dark waters. Our boat progressed slowly, and this display continued in the mist, sometimes clearer to the eyes than others. Ghat after ghat, the Indians celebrated the river and themselves. Washing, chanting, praying . . . it was still and peaceful.

This was a ritual of gratitude, I figured, a Hindu celebration of all of life. I temporarily forgot the gnawing desperation of the beggar children, and I felt the urgency of grabbing hold of life and rising above the muck so we might know our own goodness and our connection to the divine. The banks were dense with people breathing brilliant color, joy, and life force through the mist. I took photo after photo, knowing they could never capture this passionate human mosaic, as my fellow travelers stared off into the distance with their mask-like faces.

For so many, the Ganges lies at the end of the pilgrimage; Indians journey here continually from all parts of this vast country to bathe, wash clothing, celebrate, or to die and be cremated here. Those who come often carry away the sacred mud of the Ganges in brass vessels, and because journeys are always circular, they return with the ashes of loved ones to deposit them in "Mother Ganga." I noticed one of the cremation ghats, Manikarnika, smoldering quietly as our boat passed, the pyre holding the fire within until a new corpse arrived. Most of our group looked away, I noticed. I imagined Manikarnika always burning, alive and ready. The fire that breaks us down is intrinsic energy, perpetual and red at the center, and on this gray damp morning, the wisps of cremation smoke comforted me, reminding me of our ongoing journey. I never did see an actively burning pyre or ritual immersion of a corpse into the river, but I felt complete and at home as I breathed in the smoky air surrounding this place. In the Hindu mind, we are not on a journey from life to death, but rather we are making a mysterious transition from life to life. It is all about transition . . . I was beginning to see things just a bit differently now both inside and out.

Everything that arises passes away. In dense fog on the Ganges, I saw that everything we witness is impermanent, like the sticks of camphor and heavy sweet incense that burn forever in the temples of the south, disappearing as they smolder, or the garlands of brilliant yellow marigolds draped over Ganesha and Hanuman that eventually wither and die in all the temples. The shifting and changing of color and form is beautiful and as mysterious as death. I was sure I could see the people's joy on the river banks, and then it would be swallowed and there would be soupy grayness, moisture everywhere, green-black stagnant river water below with the flock of little burning candles winking at us. What did these little lights signify? They seemed like quiet little prayers to me.

As I reimagine this beautiful scene, I remember a curious word that stuck in my mind from an earlier conversation on the tour: accretive. On one of our very long bus trips, our guide, Olivier, told us that Hinduism was an "accretive" religion that essentially swallowed up other practices and blended them into its own. This was his oversimplified answer to my persistent query on the road, my burning question: Why had Buddhism pretty much disappeared from India, its sacred birthplace? It turns out that there was a pretty dark historical reason for the disappearance: the Muslims' cruel campaign to push conversion to their religion, as they laid siege to India in the early 1500s, burning Buddhist monasteries, libraries, and universities. Had Buddhism not been weakened in this way, it probably would not have been so easily absorbed by the Hindu tradition.

Over 2500 years ago, there was an Indian prince named Siddhartha Gautama with a driving need to understand the truth of human life, and he became a teacher of his people. He demonstrated that the cornerstones of a good life were wisdom, compassion, and non-harming, and he dared to propose that there was no division among beings, and no separate intrinsic human form ("form is emptiness, emptiness is form"). He lived a long life traveling the countryside and changing people's lives. His radical teachings eventually faded from the Indian culture, as the sprawling Hindu religion, with its pantheon of male and female and animal gods, became dominant, ultimately explaining to the devotees that the Buddha was simply a reincarnation of Vishnu. Over time, most of the Buddhist temples crumbled and were abandoned, some to be redecorated later with Hindu deities. The painted caves of Ajanta and sculptures of Ellora in central India are elegant examples of the marriage of these two spiritual paths. So, today's tourists find themselves staring into a jumbled, quirky mix of Buddhist and Hindu aesthetic while touring the temples and shrines throughout this vast country. Buddhas, Nandis (cows) and Ganeshas (elephants), Parvatis, Shivas, Hanumans (monkeys), Avalokitesvara . . . Where are we really? What land is this? Good question. As best we can, we must make our way mindfully and patiently in India through the discordant, exquisite kaleidoscope of spiritual art and tradition and mind-bending human drama, so we may understand the fragility and impermanence of all things and salute the divine in all our fellow beings. Namaste!

Seven: Falling in Love with Elephants in Kenya

Seventeen years ago, I went on my first safari in East Africa, and the words of a close friend—"It will transform your life"—came true. I fell in love with the infinite landscape, the warm and generous people, the lions, rhinos, impala, and the cheetahs. But mostly I fell for the elephant, the highly evolved ancient animal of epic form whose heart and gentleness broke me wide open. When I flew away from Tanzania that summer in the late nineties, I carried inside the stinging smell of the grasses, the sad poetic beauty of the lion kill, the menacing yet comic movement of the hyenas, bright orange sunsets, the goofiness of a giraffe in movement, and the loving maternal character of the elephant. I was convinced I had discovered something I had been searching for all my life.

Lewa Downs—Kenya—1997—The First Look

What I saw first through the camera lens was a vast gritty gray landscape with ruts, hills, and valleys of wrinkled hide all coated with dust. Then I noticed generous feathery eyelashes protecting her thoughtful eyes. I put the camera down and looked into the eyes of a giant elephant matriarch who stood watching our group of safari travelers from about twenty-five feet away. I don't think any of us in the car had ever seen a creature so vast, gentle, and well-meaning. She stood in the road staring at us, that's all, very calm and collected. We were crammed in our dusty Land Rover, all six of us firing questions quietly at Iain, our safari guide, as our driver stopped the car and the momma elephant held her ground. It was, as it turned out, a rare opportunity to experience an elephant this close. Up to now, we had been witnessing the wandering elephant families in the distance, small herds of eight or ten with the babies always kept inside their protective circle. It came as no surprise that elephants are in the habit of avoiding humans, about whom they must have a healthy skepticism. The elephant's memory is legendary—it is true that they rarely forget—and alive in their collective memory are the incidents of subjugation for work and entertainment (think of the circus, for one), and most importantly the many thousands of massacres over the centuries in the service of the ivory market.

Our newfound ally swayed her monstrous head from side to side, her long trunk moving gracefully as though to music. We could hear her breathing and snorting, and the fierce crunch of branches. These 14,000-pound beasts are gentle and graceful for their enormous size; they move on the ground with a light touch, their massive stump-like feet meeting the earth's dust soundlessly. Though I had, of course, planned to take hundreds of stunning close-ups of the elephants of East Africa, I knew this morning that I needed to set aside my camera and face this inquisitive pachyderm directly. No filters. Just two female faces regarding one another; it took my breath away. I could detect the details in her long dark gray lashes and the swarming community of flies that surrounded her noble and unperturbed face. Feathery acacia leaves still hung from her mouth that seemed to be smiling at us. When I later pursued my study of elephants, I learned that they possess another interesting human characteristic other than intelligence and friendliness, and that is forgiveness. It has been rumored that they are able to forgive and trust most human beings who come in curiosity and in peace. Perhaps *letting go* is a better way of putting it. It seemed that this female and the others of her tribe were able, in this moment, to let go of their dark historical memory and accept a relationship with us.

As in those rare and magical moments of falling head over heels, when all surrounding phenomena fade before our eyes, I was caught in a bubble and lost connection with my fellow humans. Held by the gaze of this magnificent wise elephant face, I had no inkling of what was said then or who said it. From the back of our Land Rover, I stared intently to impress this new feeling into my mind's eye, and I felt my heart warming. This new alliance felt strangely familiar, I had known this before surely—in another lifetime perhaps? Maybe soon I can reconsider reincarnation? That ancient face, all rough and gray and worn and beautiful, had crossed over centuries of historical time and touched a timeless and hungry female part of who I was, that most intimate piece of myself that so far had not been nurtured by my newfound love and traveling companion, Charlie, for whom I had given up my marriage.

For the rest of our safari that summer, I hungered for elephants.

Amboseli Park—1997—Witnessing Death

Charlie and I were on our way back to camp with Samuel, our quiet and deep-thinking private guide, having separated from our larger safari group, when we came upon a scene both normal and extraordinary. A congregation of elephants of all sizes stood motionless around the dead body of a large female elephant, surrounded by scavengers of all shapes and sizes. In the bright midday sun, the lifeless ballooned body resembled a giant gray whale or an epic mountain rising from the dirt. Greasy-looking black vultures swooped and hovered and swooped again, pecking away at the sour-smelling carcass; they shrieked nervously, and the hyenas did their slinking dance around the dead elephant. From the very first time I laid eyes on hyenas in Africa, I couldn't figure out whether they were truly ugly or sadistically comical. I remember not being able to find words in my mind when I first saw the dead elephant and her entourage, but Charlie managed to fill up the silence with a series of routine questions about elephant behavior. Gentle Samuel brought our Land Rover to a halt so we could begin to study the scene. I must have asked questions, such as the most important one of all: did she die naturally, or was she murdered? "This is an old age death . . . you see her tusks are still there, and there's no blood," he told me softly, his words barely audible, "and don't forget our long drought here," he offered, reminding us of nature's indifference on the African plain. Yes, I noticed an absence of violence here—bjust a complete quiet and emptiness. I felt relieved that she had died as a part of the unfolding of things in the bush, but what felt extraordinary to me at the moment was the large congregation of elephants who stood in a circle in attendance to the deceased.

I had never before seen animals bear witness and mourn

the dead. They were still and silent, including the smaller young elephants, as they held the space for a member of their family. Before I came on safari, I had been reading about the all-embracing nature of the elephant herd, how all the choices and activities of the group are determined by the need *to preserve the family*; this behavior went deeper and stretched beyond our (my) own current limited human understanding. I could see, in this moment of witnessing, that the loss of this particular elephant was a severe blow to the family she traveled with, and I felt a tugging in my chest and some warm tears falling down my face. It was possible she was the leader of her tribe, and most importantly *the carrier of their social consciousness*, and now another senior female would have to rise up to take care of the herd. Community, intelligence, and love affirmed.

We had been staying at Amboseli National Park for a few days now and had gone on a couple of long game drives with Samuel while he taught us about the complex elephant culture, and the tireless human efforts to protect these animals from illegal poaching, one of Africa's darkest historical realities. Vast amounts of money stream into the country from the sale of elephant tusks as the Chinese commercial interests continue to be intoxicated by the acquisition and the money-making possibilities of ivory. The craving and greed have corrupted many intelligent and righteous organizations that once had a mission and responsibility to stop the massacre of African elephants, which occurs these days at a shocking rate of one elephant every half hour, while in other parts of the world, we humans move through our lives minding our own business. At the foot of Mt. Kilimanjaro, on a vast plain that spreads out from south to west, an American woman named Moss created a sanctuary for elephants, both a refuge and study center where all efforts were devoted to the safety and preservation of their lives. Cynthia Moss started the Amboseli Elephant Trust more than thirty years ago to chronicle the lives and deaths of literally thousands of elephants in this part of Kenya, describe their family structure, track their movements, and keep them protected; she and her research assistants have worked tirelessly to raise awareness of their fragile place in the landscape where rule of law prevails only minimally, and greed perverts some of the best conservation plans. Her work continues valiantly today.

Parts of this noble female's face had been eaten away, but her long tusks were still visible, lying all creamy white and lifeless on the ground. How long the grief congregation of her companions would stay I had no clue, nor could Samuel tell us. We had to embrace the unknown here. They would be in attendance until there was no longer the need, until their grief was spent and mourning came to a close in its own time. Then they would resume the rhythm of their lives, begin again their march in search of food and water, although they would return here eventually to fondle and collect the bones of their comrade, and carry them along with them. We humans put the remains of the dead in an urn or a wooden box and then in the ground, but the elephants take their beloved ones along on their forward journey for an indeterminate amount of time, cradling (caressing) the fragments close to their huge bodies . . . with love.

Loisaba, Kenya—2010—Boundaries Defined

On what felt to me like a sacred pilgrimage, I returned to East Africa thirteen years later with my youngest daughter and her family—to share and to touch again the magic of the animals in the wild, and perhaps find transformation.

We were bumping along on a morning game drive with our guide, Lenny, a lanky, grinning Samburu man, searching for rare wild dogs, when we came upon a group of the elusive little deer-like creatures called dik-diks with their enormous black eyes on tiny pointed faces, who prance and cavort rather than run, and who mate for life. They seemed so portable and as whimsical as fairytale animals. Grinning happily about our latest sighting and humming to himself, Lenny barreled along the narrow road winding back and forth to return us to our lodge for lunch. There were huge lush trees on the right and open space to the left.

Suddenly a great rustling and swooshing, and a trio of female elephants emerged through the foliage, towering over it and marching deliberately toward us, crushing branches as they came. Standing in the Rover with our heads poking out of the open roof, we could see their giant ears flapping rapidly—hardly a sign of tranquility or ease. They trumpeted and rumbled as their huge bodies swayed from side to side. The trumpeting was a terrifying sound, like a dark frightened roar from the center of the earth. Lenny put on the brakes quickly and we started to catch our breath. There clearly was no running off for us: there were pictures to be taken, of course, and a fabulous close view from our secure automobile! But then it happened. The ground began to pulse as these disturbed females charged toward us. We dropped our cameras but kept looking back as Lenny gunned the Rover's engine to get us away from there. I compulsively picked up my camera one last time to capture an image and noticed then that there was a small baby among them, the one all the agitation was about. We had traversed their territory without knowing, as the large gray females lurked unseen in the brush. Baby elephants, as it turns out, are nurtured by many mothers, known as "allomothers," the aunts and older sisters and other unrelated females of the tribe. We had come too close to this clan, and it was time to depart—quickly. Our guy got our car in gear and started to pick up speed as the road began to climb, and the elephants, after a brief chase, stopped and stood perfectly still, watching us curiously as we moved away with our hearts racing,

The sight of the huge females charging out of the bushes, dwarfing all they confronted, made me think in a quick moment of a widescreen dinosaur movie where humans who had suddenly been transformed into miniature creatures were about to end up in the clutches of the giant animals who ruled the land. We had crossed over a line that we could not see. Almost fallen down the rabbit hole. Not understood the way through the landscape. Lenny laughed nervously and shouted, "Eh, how about that, that was kind of scary, wasn't it, man?" He wasn't smiling now. I could hear that he was voicing not only our feelings, but his own as well. In the African bush, man doesn't make the rules or really know the way. And you don't ever negotiate with a matriarch who is busy doing her job, protecting her family.

Who Protects Whom?—Yellow Springs and Las Vegas, 1966

Before the light came up on that bitter cold January morning in Ohio, I left my house north of town where my husband and daughter of one and a half years slept soundly, and I drove away. I was headed for glittering Las Vegas, a surreal place in the Nevada desert where I thought I might reassemble my identity with a young man whose eyes and hair were dark and whose smile was crooked, but who promised to adore me and give me all the respect I had been missing in my marriage.

"I can make you happy, I know I can. Because I respect you," Bob promised through the cigarette smoke, and I believed him. In that moment.

I had been wallowing, feeling lost and not seen in my young marriage. Jack married me because he had to—it was the early sixties, and it wasn't the right time for safe abortions, and I was only nineteen and lacked the courage and ability to take care of a baby on my own. And so, I leaned on the good will of my future father-in-law who had a surprising affection for me, and he in turn ordered his son Jack to "do the right thing" late one evening as he sipped his whisky in a local steakhouse. My mother-in-law was so angry that she announced she wouldn't attend the wedding, but finally gave in and showed up wearing a trim little dark suit and a tight countenance. Surrounded by a small contingent of college friends and our awkward family members, we read the words we had written for each other in a cozy Quaker chapel on campus on a cold January afternoon in 1965.

On our wedding day, Jack actually muttered to one of his school friends that he didn't expect the marriage to last very long, but it would be years later before I ever heard about that unkindness. I dropped out of school for the second time so I could handle marriage and motherhood and figure out how to live in the same house with my husband's roommates, while Jack was able to cruise on toward his degree in physics. I then suffered through an oppressive summer in southeastern Ohio, waiting for the arrival of my baby, who was taking her time in showing up. On the day she was finally born, I had actually been recruited to help move our furnishings from one apartment to the other—an unpleasant, undignified, and I thought unwise assignment for someone in my condition, but preferable to being prostrated in some uncomfortable chair trying to will my child's arrival into being.

After an initial period of wordless joy, there were many months of disjointed conversations, slamming doors, and loud arguments while the baby slept in her crib, too much drinking, and for myself a lurking and unexpressed fear that I had taken on more than I could ever handle. We had embarked on what seemed like a simulation of marriage: I did the laundry, cooked food, and kept house—sort of—and then came the diapers, sore breasts, and baby food, and off he went to his new job. When he wasn't working, he was experimenting with drugs.

That first Christmas we spent together, he gave me an electric can opener as a present, a soulless gift to be sure, and all because kitchen gadgets were the kind of gifts his mother had always expected from his father. For a while, I made dark jokes about all the reasons this was the wrong present for me, and eventually I stopped because no one was listening. I was not heard. We went through our days playing our parts in a large high-ceilinged house north of town with lots of dark paneled walls and not enough light to help me feel cheerful. I didn't drive, had few friends, and was lonely. I was not seen . . . except by this squirming and helpless little child who looked at me with her huge brown eyes. What was needed in that very moment? How could I possibly tell? Was my heart starting to break then from the confusion and fright I felt?

When I left our house that night of my escape, I wrote a note that said I was going "somewhere warm," and I did not name the place; I wanted to disappear. I also wrote that I was sure that he would find a way take good care of our daughter; he would because now he had to. On the morning of January 25th, I took money from our bank account in town on the way to the airport, and boarded an American Airlines plane for Nevada, carrying just a few winter clothes with me. Robert and I drank a couple of Bloody Marys on the plane and talked idly about how good the adventure was going to be. I tried not to picture the sleeping child in her bed, or to think about all the friends and family who would certainly judge me for slinking away from home in the dark of night. When we arrived in the dry heat of Las Vegas, we made a beeline for the Dunes Hotel on the Strip, checked into a room, and I headed straight for the gift shop to buy bright colored Capri pants and gold lamé slippers. I was determined to try on a new persona.

A few days into the experience I found myself writing this in my journal:

> The Dunes Hotel lobby screamed slots, and neon, and cheap red velvet curtains. . . . Made up cocktail waitresses in tight little yellow skirts slink through the crowd holding trays loaded with drinks. Instinctively, I head toward the poker tables. . . . Back there in memory lurked some funky romance with poker. . . . What else was there to do? Here I was, lost in Las Vegas, a runaway from my husband and child, and all I want is to forget. Forget where I come from, forget who I am with, forget that my daughter back home is only one and a half years old.
>
> I hover by the table and soon figure out this is too big a game for the likes of me. I don't have the savvy or the poker face. The Blackjack table looks more user-friendly. I sidle up with my fistful of red chips and take note of the sullen dealer with a greasy visor and the motley players sitting at their perches. The monotonous clacking of chips is hypnotic, and the bright glare of the fluorescent ceiling lights hurts my head—or was that the three Bloody Marys I had on the plane ride here?
>
> I glance down at the sparkly gold lamé shoes and neon-colored capris I had just purchased at the hotel gift

shop, desperately willing myself to become someone else. Trying to disappear? Or had I already disappeared? This vast room is a maze of people of all sizes and shapes who are betting on another chance—like I was. There are no clocks on any wall, no windows; we are caught in a dark, timeless, and faceless landscape, feeding our fears and distractions. . . .

And then he moves up behind me and breathes his hot breath in my ear, and says, "Hey, sweetheart, I brought you something!" He holds out a giant wet martini with three green olives, and he grins like someone who had just gotten away with murder.

Back in Yellow Springs, my husband read the note early in the morning, and reeling from confusion, called upon the only person he could imagine would help him: my mother, who then lived in Manhattan. Soon enough, he bundled up Tara and boarded a plane for JFK and found his way to her brightly lit Greenwich Village apartment. He was looking for answers and comfort, and figured she was his best bet to discover my whereabouts. My narcissistic mother, who had never demonstrated an interest in mothering, who'd farmed me out to family and parked me with babysitters, who had ignored me until it was time to dress me up for the senior dance in shiny purple satin, smoke cigarettes, and send me off to college, was now being asked to provide protection and safety for her only grandchild and son-in-law. And so, she did. A playpen was purchased, a crib and toys and books, and many long talks unfolded late into the evenings over drinks about how things would turn out all right in the end, that I would eventually come to my senses and give up this strange fantasy. She kept assuring him that I would return because I would have to—there was the issue of money after all—and if I didn't return on my own, she would use the necessary measures to force the issue; she clearly knew something about me that I didn't know myself.

Was she trying to make up for all the years of turning away, when I was eating myself into obesity, feeling terrified of not being pretty in high school, when I needed tender care and holding rather than a shrink to label me as a rebellious teenage alcoholic? Much later in our lives, she told me she had been a bad mother and knew it, and I demurred. I didn't want to say outright what was in my heart—that would hurt too much—and I wasn't very good with anger. Now it appeared she was starting a new script, and when I later learned that my little family had been under her wing while I sleepwalked in Las Vegas, I was strangely comforted that she was becoming the unlikely matriarch.

I lasted about ten days on this odyssey with the dark-haired Robert, who had a bit of a gambling problem, ate and drank too much, and smoked in bed; money began disappearing, and I needed to call for help. I had been having disturbing dreams about little Tara, alone in a New York apartment, and my angry confused husband, and all the steak dinners and martinis I consumed did not help. I felt an aching panic inside: I had gone too far this time, but I was sure Mom would rescue me. After all, she was my mother, she had to be on my side (ancient notions die hard!). When I told her where I was and said I needed money, she told me I'd have to meet her conditions: meet Jack in Las Vegas and begin to grasp what I had done. She was pointing the way out of my little trap. I couldn't continue to run, she said; one simply didn't abandon one's children. As I heard that, I felt a strange relief and a letting go. And then too there was that haunting image in my head again and again of the child who was lying in her porta-crib on West 12th Street with a hard-drinking grandma and no mother. I realized how very tired I was, so sick and tired of pretending I was someone who could escape and find happiness.

It would all end in Las Vegas in keeping with my mother's conditions: a meeting in the hotel coffee shop with my stricken husband, a stirring of my heart for my little daughter, the heavy judgment I carried for leaving her behind, and some fragile plans to pick up the pieces and try to rebuild our family life. As Jack and I talked of these plans over lukewarm coffee, my boyfriend, who was lying in our hotel room smoking, decided it was time to pack his suitcase, carefully tucking away the pistol he had brought with him (why had this not been a clue about his unreliability?). He was hoping to bow out gracefully, retrieve some dignity, I imagine, but I hardly remember anything about that. All I could think of was finding an anchor in my husband's love again, and in my child's need for me. I reminded myself to thank my mother for becoming a protector for one of the few times in her life.

Amboseli Park, Kenya—2010—In Community

It was our last day exploring elephant country, and I nudged Juma to take us one last time to find more elephants. My family wanted this, I told him, but I suspect he knew all along that it was really all about what I wanted. It seemed I could never get my fill of these massive animals. We piled into the Land Rover and left Amboseli Park, where we were staying, so we might drive off-road for a change. Beautiful marshes stretched out before us, green reeds and grasses and irises and elegant white water birds and pink flamingos. . . . The road got bumpier and bumpier as we careened along off in the direction our driver clearly had good feelings about. He hadn't even needed binoculars to detect a large herd of elephants huddled far off on a large plateau beyond the swampy marshland, and that's where we were headed.

"Can we make it up there, really?" I asked eagerly.

"Think so," said he. Juma, like a couple of the other Kenyan guides we had traveled with, was not a very verbal character; they're all far too busy paying attention to the landscape and wildlife to indulge in casual conversation. And off he sped, skillfully navigating the rolling terrain, as we held on to anything that would keep us steady in the car, the three grandkids grinning widely at the adventure of it all.

Pretty soon the mass of giant gray figures became much larger and more distinct, and before I knew it, we had motored right into the midst of the herd itself. Not one of my family spoke—whether they were terrified or speechlessly excited, I couldn't tell. I do remember my daughter mumbling something about was it okay for us to be getting in this close, and would the elephants be upset? Juma was undaunted, and pretty soon he brought the car to a stop in the middle of the community of beasts. We were now surrounded by a huge circle of elephants who were continuing about their business pretty much unfazed. All we could hear was the snapping and tearing of the grasses from the earth, some soft grunts and rumbling sounds, and then the incessant clicking of cameras as we pivoted ourselves this way and that to capture the mass of animals around us. Even my young grandson Cal was uncharacteristically quiet. He knew the adventure was a new and mysterious one.

I smelled salty funky foliage that reminded me of rivers and swamps, and the sweet earthy smell of dung. Far away, some birds called out to each other. There were young elephants everywhere in the crowd, from the one-month-old who wobbled on his small stumpy legs and flailed his uncoordinated little trunk about, to the juveniles, about two years and up, who were midsize and moving their bodies confidently, still watching their mothers. They were obviously in training to keep an eye on the very young. This herd was primarily female. Soon we noticed one lone male marching toward our circle with some flourish and dust swirling, his giant dark penis swaying wildly as he approached, his mammoth head held high. His step was heavy and pounding; you could hear him on the ground, and his breath was heaving as he marched. He was, Juma pointed out, in search of a mate, and before long had separated out one of the smaller females and chased her away from the herd. In order to conduct his mating ritual properly, he had to take his chosen female away from her group. Rules of the game, elephant etiquette. When I learned about the solitary lives of the males, I felt sorry for them; they generally left the female community into which they were born at about age six, and from there pursued a lonely path in life, driven by certain conditions to fight for territory and, of course, to mate when the females were ready. They certainly lived without the familial comforts of the herd.

Here at Amboseli, our surrounding herd continued to amble in what looked like slow motion, many of them keeping their eyes on us, and we remained suspended in time. I felt some anxiety here and there, a low level of fear, I suspect, and at the same time I was giddy with the excitement of being so close to these gentle giants. I wondered what it would feel to stand right next to one of these massive beasts, so close you could feel the warmth radiate from their bodies and look deeply into the rough gray landscape of their hides and feel safe. Sadly, the edge between safety and the great unknown was a frail one. Too much dark history, too little time. . . . The afternoon was getting on now, and more elephants milled about, eating and grunting, with little white birds perched on their huge backs, and their trunks swaying rhythmically in soft sunlight. Life was unfolding. The grandchildren were still quiet; were they anxious, or just lost in their own imaginations and future plans? Juma was looking pretty smug as he watched in silence from the driver's seat. In some ways, it felt as though time had stopped: there was no tomorrow, no hotel, and no airplane taking us away to America. There was the green marsh and the birds and the elephants. We human beings were becoming less and less visible in the landscape, it seemed, fading into the long continuum of life in the wild. I tried to take pictures and seize that feeling of being surrounded by these elephants, but of course it could not be captured. How can you take hold of a living, breathing container that has no visible boundaries, that is so mutable?

We must have stayed put with our elephant friends for an hour and a half, speaking only in whispers, and when we cautiously began to drive away, I felt a heavy weight in my heart, the kind you feel when you say goodbye—*really* goodbye—to someone you deeply love. Some of them watched our retreat through their long lashes, but mostly we were ignored, again. I looked back as we bumped on down the marshy roads for home, trying to etch the scene in my mind and heart: the sights (wobbly little babies nursing happily, males courting), sounds (the gentle grunts and chewing and the birds cooing), the soft footfalls, and the love all around.

Eight: On Not Knowing Vietnam

The Tomb of Uncle Ho and Ancestor Worship

On an overcast and pleasantly cool morning, I joined the parade of serious, reverent visitors who marched silently in single file for several blocks toward the monolithic granite mausoleum of Ho Chi Minh in the heart of Hanoi. Again, I felt alone among the Vietnamese, and I noticed how inherently sober the whole process felt. All this sobriety made me want to wave my arms, act like a little kid, or otherwise put some of my own quirkiness out into the world.

I was an inherently well-behaved soul, so I just kept noting this ordered and somewhat soulless landscape. Then there was the usual irreverent chatter in my head about the strangeness of the monument, the overbearing formality of the process, and the whole unfathomable notion of preserving a human body intact for over thirty years. All the mausoleum visitors had their arms at their sides and spoke in hushed voices if at all. Duang, my guide, relieved me of my camera and left me off at the beginning of the procession, and I knew I wouldn't see him again until I had viewed the body and exited from the building. I felt a bit abandoned and oddly naked without the camera that had become my go-between as I traveled through all the unfamiliar little streets in Asia. My camera gives me an identity, after all, and eventually becomes a shield from the piercing gaze of those you visit. So, with no one to converse with now, I felt deprived of yet another prop.

Uncharacteristically, I had done little homework on Ho Chi Minh, but I did know that while he was a revolutionary who made the whole world pay attention back in the sixties, he was in fact a humble personality with simple tastes, for whom this kind of chauvinistic display might have been distasteful. I passed several perfect formations of young soldiers in stiff white uniforms standing guard outside, all of their very young faces lacking any expression. Once inside the building and up some stairs, I entered the sanctum with its glass bier holding the thirty-year-old corpse of the North Vietnamese hero dressed in his trademark khaki suit all pressed and clean. It was icy cold in this cavernous space, as though we had all just stepped into a refrigerator. He died in 1969 and was placed in this perpetual state by a government that boldly ignored his wishes to be cremated. I could have sworn that he had just recently laid himself down to rest, an afternoon nap perhaps, his slim little hands crossed at the waist and illuminated from a chilly white light focused his way, his sparse white beard clean and perfectly groomed; his face looked gentle to me with just the right amount of life in it. I wanted to ask someone, "How do they do that . . . make him look so alive?" but of course there wasn't a soul to ask.

We marched around his reclining figure, no one saying a word, no cameras clicking, just the quiet shuffling of feet. I tried to slow myself down to get a longer view of the man so I could imprint the strangeness of the sight on my memory: this legendary man revered in Asia and hated in the West for over fifty years now lay before us looking more or less fresh and alive, while the Vietnamese people from the countryside moved by passively, as though transported on some moving sidewalk. Solemnity hung in the air, but there was no hint of ardor or faith on the visitors' faces. I felt again that spooky distance—is it cultural or emotional?—that I sometimes feel when I seek to understand Asian habits and views. I have a hard time connecting all the puzzle pieces in front of me. I kept wondering to myself why all these people were here.

Outside the dour stone building I found Duang, and I told him this was one of the most unforgettable sights I had seen in all my travels. "I've never seen anything quite this amazing . . . I'm thrilled with how *weird* it is!" I declared, slapping my hand on my thigh as I made the proclamation and smiling. He seemed surprised and a bit confused by my outspokenness, and then went on to tell me in his official "guide-speak" voice that during the months of September and October, the venerable Ho cannot be viewed, because that is the time he is flown to Moscow to be treated. I think that was the exact word he used: "treated." Did my young guide not think this was a strange fact, that his government spent large sums of money to preserve the former leader when a large portion of his fellow countrymen suffered in poverty? I don't remember hearing a response to the question, which probably means I never asked him, but simply thought the thought and pondered the strangeness. I certainly wondered what old "Uncle Ho," as he is affectionately called, would have thought of this spectacle. We went on then to visit the park nearby where Ho's cozy and humble little house was nestled, and this simple wooden cabin gave me a very different view of the man who seemed to have had modest tastes and a quiet view of life. I bought a book about him and his politics featuring a stern black-and-white portrait on the cover, again looking for something tangible that I could hold on to.

Ho's mausoleum was a heavy and grim structure inspired by the Soviets' monument to Lenin, built on Ba Dinh Square in central Hanoi, where Ho Chi Minh had proclaimed Vietnamese independence in 1945 and taken his place on the world stage. The Communist Party finished the project in 1975 and had their leader embalmed by the Russians so he could be lodged in this newly created "temple" to enjoy eternal regard and respect. Such was the ideal. While a steady flow of visitors came to witness—mainly folks from outside the cities—there seemed to be an abiding ambivalence or indifference in the country and elsewhere about whether this man was a patriot or just a willful socialist revolutionary. The sweep of history seems to have dulled whatever adulation existed, and he has joined Vietnam's perpetually receding past that is now dominated by a contradictory mix of murky communist ideology and capitalist drive.

As Duang and I marched from the mausoleum to the park and Ho's house, I mulled over the question: why keep the earthly body going? And what do all the thousands who come to file by his corpse really think? I walked alongside this young man whose connection to his own past seemed slim, who wore stylish blue jeans and carried a shiny smartphone, and he did not talk of history or culture or politics. He stuck to his business of shepherding the tourist lady from the West to all the appointed places, treating her respectfully but viewing her with minimal curiosity. No doubt he texted and listened to music and worried about buying a new TV, looking into the future instead of the past. He was a child of a new and different time, freed from the stories of what came before. And so, I remained once more in the dark.

In so many of the temples I visited with my various young guides in Vietnam, I noticed the giant carved, brightly painted ancestor gods standing at the entrance or around the perimeter of the sanctum where incense and prayers were offered. They stood over eight feet in height and looked menacing, their bright red-and-gold paint jobs dingy with smoke. They wore fierce expressions, they gnashed their teeth, and their eyes told you to be on your guard. They certainly didn't suggest any welcoming to me as I walked past. I recalled a much earlier trip to China and visits to various shrines that housed similar warrior figures everywhere in the same red-and-gold, always surrounded by the swirling smoke of incense and mystery. Was there such a thing as a distinctly Vietnamese temple, I asked Duang, and he informed me that what I saw was indeed Vietnamese. The intimate and long relationship between China and Vietnam seemed to be a logical enough reason for the overlay of the Chinese aesthetic onto Vietnamese culture.

In both Chinese and Vietnamese temples, I saw altars dedicated to the ancestors, places where photographs of family members were placed along with flowers, tangerines, containers of incense, and small trinkets of remembrance. As I understood it, when someone goes to the pagoda to pay respects to the elders and offer food and incense, he or she thereby secures their place in daily life, essentially keeping them alive in the present. The older generation—those who have moved through old age and died—seem to be taking an indefinite rest in their midst, holding their place in the land of the living.

There has been a long history of ancestor worship here and in China, and I'm reminded again of Ho Chi Minh's preserved human form that creates an eerie illusion of human presence in our time. Would the Vietnamese today forget this national hero if it weren't for the surreal cold tomb in Hanoi where people show up month after month to pay attention?

Well-loved travel writer Paul Theroux recently commented in an interview that the reason he journeyed continually was that it was a way for him to understand who he is in the world, how he fits into the larger complex and exotic environments he visits. When I first began to travel to foreign countries, inspired by my three childhood years living in Italy, I'm sure my intention was just to hear the stories, become educated, and soak up the culture. It wasn't until I began all this looking back at the traveling life that I understood that my journeying was about understanding who I was in a variety of different landscapes. I needed to understand how I fit into the larger world.

In most of my Vietnam experiences in that winter of 2013, I discovered that I felt uncomfortable being solitary, and I became lost in my own thinking about this place I assumed I could fathom in a few weeks. My own confusion in the thought process, or more elegantly put in the Korean Zen tradition, "Don't Know Mind," felt a little like being lost here and there, and this has unsettled my hardworking ego that is driven to find answers. Of course, unsettling the ego, from the Buddhist perspective, is the whole point. This "stranger in a strange land" feeling can be disorienting, yes, but I believe it's key to the traveler's path to gain insight in places where they don't speak your language. When I allow this not knowing to just be and let go of fear, I find an increased spaciousness of mind, and a flood of questions arises, which of course leads to more searching and learning. And all that makes my introverted self quite happy. I had that sort of experience when I visited Ho's tomb and the mysterious smoky temples secured by the forbidding guardians. I was simply at the beginning of a long journey of inquiry that had an uncertain end.

Fear and Loathing in Golden Gate Park—1967

I remember now a surreal day in the summer of 1967, a remarkable and historic time when young hippies by the thousands invaded the San Francisco landscape, and my husband and I had just moved to the city. By some inexplicable set of circumstances, my husband Jack's ex-girlfriend was visiting us from the East, and I recall a lot of cigarette smoking and staying up late and talking in code about the good old days at Antioch College. Judith had thick dark eyebrows, wiry unkempt hair, big teeth, and a perpetual grimace. I never figured out what he saw in her. I had never prided myself on being a beauty—how could I, growing up next to my mother who had movie-star good looks when she was a young woman?—and then there was Jack's cruel wisecrack about marrying me for my mind, not my looks . . . but I held on to a mean-spirited opinion that Judith Etkind was one of the homelier girls I had ever seen. Try as I might not to think about the nature of this past relationship, I continued to wonder.

He wanted to show her a good time while she was visiting the city, and it happened we were living then in the midst of a revolutionary counterculture movement everyone called "The Summer of Love." San Francisco was awash in patchouli oil, cheap incense, hordes of scruffy wide-eyed young people in rumpled Indian cottons, and wildly good rock 'n' roll blasting from airwaves and apartment windows and parks, and of course, hanging over all of this the tangy perfume of marijuana. So, what better to do with your visitor from a different part of the country than go to Golden Gate Park and do some drugs? "We have some old acid stored in the freezer, that ought to do it," Jack cheerfully remarked.

A picnic was organized with beer and wine and probably some deli sandwiches. I had been fearful for quite a while of this new LSD experience that transformed people into scrambled, spaced out, goofy characters, but on this particular day I felt game and ready to show the old flame that I could indulge in the serious stuff with the rest of the gang. It appeared that there was only enough acid for two people, and I made a point to take the plunge with this woman I didn't trust. Jack would abstain because he'd be taking care of our two-year-old daughter Tara, and a few of our other friends would join in simply for the fun of going to the park on a sunny afternoon. Standing in our high-ceilinged kitchen on Potrero Hill, I looked at the small amount of white powder in the plastic bag from the freezer and found it hard to believe that anything would come of it. Jack said to me, "I've given Judy some of this . . . here, take the rest of it—we've had it for a long time . . . probably not very strong anymore." And so I did, feeling uncharacteristically brave.

The next thing I remember is sitting in Sharon Meadow in Golden Gate Park as the sun dappled the green around us, stretching out on a blanket surrounded by coolers and jackets and potato chip bags, and watching my daughter play Frisbee with Harry, an old college friend. In a blue-checkered dress, she bounced happily from side to side as though on springs, her little arms reaching up for the Frisbee, her beautiful brown curls framing chubby pink cheeks. The ex-girlfriend had wandered off to take a walk, and we sat on the blanket while Jack drank a beer and we talked about how easy and sweet our daughter was. Responsible, well-behaved, and steady, just as I used to be, I thought ironically. What is this thing about goodness in kids? Is it an innate quality or does it show up in order to make life easier?

She came running up to me, saying, "Mommy, Mommy," and her little face then transformed before my eyes from a beautiful and tangible cherubic countenance to something fluid and surreal: her eyelashes became huge peacock feathers, wild green and purple and blue, all lit up by the sunlight. "Mommy, Mommy, Mommy," she squealed as I sat frozen in place, waiting for the surreal feeling to go away. I tried to reach out to her and it was as though everything, including myself, was moving in horribly slow motion. A small moment in time now stretched wide like a rubber band. I wanted to tell her how beautiful she was, but I couldn't make my mouth work. Words wouldn't come . . . it felt a bit as though I'd had a stroke. She spun off suddenly to find the lost Frisbee, and I felt myself falling away from her and our friends, and I remember there were rainbows arcing through the sky, even though the fog was now starting to roll in through the eucalyptus trees. I felt strangely aphasic and was falling down Alice's rabbit hole at the same time. I began to sob, then felt like I was drowning in the tears, my body shaking with a fear I couldn't recognize right away. Crying had always seemed so unwelcome when I was a child, because when I did burst into tears in front of my mother, she barked at me, "Pull yourself together. Don't be tiresome! You need to have more of a sense of humor!" No place for my tears to land. I was not supposed to be sad. . . .

And although I sat in this beautiful moment on soft green grass in this magical park, surrounded by people I loved, I felt I was suddenly alien and was being left behind. "I'm a terrible mother, I know I am . . . I don't know how to keep her safe! I'm afraid! . . . Such a horrible mistake!" I wailed to Jack, "I'll never be able to take care of her!" This small moment of experience felt suddenly cosmic. I don't remember being reassured or supported—there were just some confused smiles coming my way—I was just floating alone. Armies of tiny insects and crawly bugs marched industriously around me in the soft dirt as the afternoon began to cool off, and I leaned over to inhale the earth and cry some more.

We eventually returned in Harry's VW bus to our tall old house on Rhode Island Street, up on a hill that faced west toward the fog-banked ocean. I have no memory of the journey home. The golden streaks in the sky now told me the sun was beginning to set out there, and I realized that Tara was in the kitchen happily devouring cookies with our friends. She was certainly safe now. . . . I watched the San Francisco streets below stretch out and undulate like snakes in the fading light, and the dread became greater. I was now in a fluid universe as the pale paint on our living room walls dripped slowly and continuously down from ceiling to floor. I was sure I had gone mad and would remain there.

It would be months before I climbed out of that rabbit hole, and even then the flickering creepy hallucinations continued at random moments, and I was still drawn to the haunting Jefferson Airplane song, "White Rabbit," particularly the line that says, "And if you go chasing rabbits, and you know you're going to fall / Tell them a hookah-smoking caterpillar has given you the call . . ." I promised myself later, around the time I became pregnant with my second child, that I would never touch acid again, that I would not go looking for Alice, no matter what the challenges to my happiness were. I remember hoping and praying in my quiet way that my small daughter would be able to forget the scary sight of her lost mother on the blanket that surreal afternoon in Golden Gate Park.

A Look at Hoa Lo Prison in Hanoi

My continuing search to unearth some truths about the Vietnam War included a visit to the notorious "Hanoi Hilton," otherwise known as Hoa Lo Prison. Duang and I drove to the French Quarter, and he let me off at the entrance to this standard destination on the tourist itinerary. This museum is a fragment of the old prison that the French built in the late 1800s and has lately become a destination not for the Vietnamese, but for countless Westerners looking for information and maybe relief from guilt for what they call here "the American War." Originally a prison where the French held and tortured Vietnamese political prisoners, it later became the holding place for the American soldiers captured by the North Vietnamese during what we have always called "the Vietnam War."

The prison is dark and claustrophobic and populated in part by numerous strangely lifelike human figures in military dress made from synthetic materials. I followed the tour route that began in a big high-ceilinged room with a guillotine once used as an instrument of execution by the French. It was a simple room, the historic guillotine was terrifying, and there was no documentation to be found, so I took it in and marched on. I thought about that room after I had left the place, and about what seemed to be the operating principle of the museum: show the visitor how well the North Vietnamese treated the Americans in contrast to the extreme suffering inflicted on them by the French. I then walked through rooms that were filled with black and white photographs of American fighting men looking young and open and quite large in comparison to their captors. Remnants of uniforms and other military memorabilia hung in glass cases, along with decks of cards, the flight suit of John McCain, and various well-worn cigarette lighters.

I paused to watch a video which depicted an odd "happy camper" scene among some of these American prisoners. I stared back into history, and saw suffering and confusion veiled by youthful camaraderie. Yes, suffering showed up in their tired eyes and the averted faces. We would never know the horrors these young soldiers witnessed long ago; they could only be revealed, if ever, in the dark of night to a loved one, or maybe a shrink, as they burned through the psyches of these men during those decades following the war. It was helpful to see the photographs, because the seeing brought some pieces of the unimaginable experience to light and helped me remember how these men, who were reviled in their own country when they returned from Vietnam, were just young boys trying their fallible best to do the right thing at this frightening moment in their country's history.

I wondered, as I walked through the prison, about how different cultures hold historical memory. In the United States, we were told that our American soldiers who were fighting the good fight were treated harshly by the Vietnamese, and it wasn't pretty—in fact, propaganda made it look as though we were the victims. Seeing this remnant of a prison suggests a broader version of this war where both sides were aggressors and both victims. When you visit here and ask your guides to talk about the war, they hesitate and perhaps share that yes, as a matter of fact, they had a father or an uncle who fought in the American War. And the conversation usually stops there. The span of the last forty years, in which the Vietnamese crawled back from humiliation and devastation to tranquil stability, has blurred the pain, the suffering, and the story from their memories.

When I was a young adult raising a family in the suburbs, I became caught up in watching the horrific television footage roaring across our little screens and felt a sadness and shame I couldn't talk about. And as the decades unfolded, I made myself watch the gritty films that Hollywood produced, and I began to associate the little country of Vietnam with a grossly out-of-balance time and a shortsighted and cruel military policy; along with thousands of others, I worried about how we as a country would recover from all those years of killing and burning. I had always wanted to see for myself the land we ravaged, the battlefields and death that the media brought so graphically into our living rooms. As far away as Vietnam was, we had an immediate voyeuristic experience that we were helpless to alter. Hauling myself and my camera through the Hoa Lo prison in 2013 felt like a weird ritual of witnessing, as I tried to attend to a piece of history I had never really known. This time I was glad that my guide wasn't with me, for I needed to move through the dark cold rooms alone, allowing the images and the claustrophobic space to play on me, much the way the Vietnamese people walked wordlessly through the mausoleum of Uncle Ho and sensed their past.

A Vietnamese Theme Park Called Chu Chi

The Chu Chi tunnels can be found twenty-one miles from Saigon, now known as Ho Chi Minh City, and represent the government's tribute to the legendary Vietnamese ingenuity as it defended against the American military forces. I sat in a bunker on a very sticky hot morning and watched a scratchy black and white propaganda film that told the story of the "American imperialists'" inhumanity. My guide had asked me earlier whether I would be offended at seeing such a diatribe against my country, and I told him I wouldn't. He didn't know, of course, that I had lived away from my country as a child and had gone to school with children from military and Foreign Service families, or that I had read the searing indictment of our foreign relations in *The Ugly American*, and had eventually become quite anti-American. The chauvinism of the Foreign Service and military kids I went to school with had made me almost embarrassed to be American. In this strange jungle landscape, as I watched the primitive little anti-American film, I realized it all felt pretty familiar.

Afterward I was taken on a walking tour of the tunnel complex, built during the war by the Vietcong, and my guide mechanically explained how the maze was created and reminded me that only very few undersized Westerners had been able to crawl through the narrow spaces to see this underground world. This cleverly designed system helped the Vietnamese survive in a heavily bombed area that was one of the few front lines in the war and the nearest base to the South Vietnamese capital city of Saigon. This was the most heavily bombed area of the entire war where close to 25,000 Vietnamese perished. I was told about the three layers at Chu Chi, with living quarters and strategy areas, and many miles of snaking routes connecting all the parts. As we walked through the sparsely wooded area and talked about the tunnels' intricate design, we came upon eerily realistic mannequins in staged configurations impersonating soldiers in battle, and we stepped carefully over lifelike mockups of the vicious trapping devices they used, cleverly camouflaged in the dirt.

The mannequins in the heat of that morning looked both real and phony, and I began to have the uncomfortable feeling I was walking through a surreal theme park in these barren woods. The Communist government, it seems, had made a conscious choice to transform this dying forest into a wartime environment filled with dioramas and weaponry exhibits to give the visiting public a view of what military life had been like. There was a toned-down hollowness to it all and a striking absence of the personal stories of the thousands who were sacrificed here. Robert Templar in his book about modern Vietnam wrote this about Chu Chi: "To shelter foreigners from the reality of war and hinder wider exploration of the past, the government offered up history in places like Chu Chi tunnels." I wondered as I left this place whether the survivors of the war might have felt betrayed by this depersonalizing of their painful history. Perhaps not. My travels through Southeast Asian countries have shown me a world where individual effort is generally minimized and the communal is revered. Individual human beings, whether heroes or just survivors, are simply part of the larger fabric of the war. The absence of personal narrative left me feeling sad. I grew up around storytellers and vast numbers of books, and I've always been a believer in personal stories; I have depended on personal narratives, in fact, to keep my bearings. This erasing of the events of a whole generation who reaped so little benefit from all their sacrifice seemed both a confusing and a wrenching error—a historical aberration.

A Suburbanite Experiences the Vietnam War— SF Bay Area—1972

The year must have been around 1972, my very grand grandmother from New York was making a special trip out to the suburbs to visit me and the family, and it just so happened that an agent of the US Treasury had recently and unexpectedly shown up to place a plain but formidable official sign on our front door that proclaimed our house in Redwood City property of the US government. Bad timing to say the least. They tacked this sign on both doors of our little suburban house, explaining in fine print that failure to pay our last two years of federal income tax was the reason for the seizure.

The Vietnam War had been raging for years, and the country was fractured and burned with dissent; I knew this primarily from watching Walter Cronkite's somber face on the CBS Evening News. I knew too that my husband Jack, who was vehemently against the war, wanted to make some statement in opposition and had convinced me that refusal to pay taxes was a great way to stand up to the government's violent campaign in Vietnam. It had all seemed fine and logical at the beginning, but now I had two formidable forces coming down on me—the US government and my grandmother—and I was unclear about what to do next.

In 1965 at the age of nineteen, I had married this man in a Quaker chapel in Yellow Springs, Ohio. I was dressed in a green A-line, he in a dark suit with a skinny tie. We recited words we had written ourselves, and two close friends held a rose and a candle. It was a quiet little alternative wedding. He was handsome in a Tony Perkins kind of way, smart and with a passion for physics, which I had no clue about. Jack had been raised in Illinois, in the heartland of the country, and he prided himself on being both a scientist and the descendant of a long line of pacifists. "No man in my family ever took up guns or went to war since well before the Civil War!" he'd proclaim proudly, and I melted with affection for this nobility. We had two beautiful daughters three years apart, a few cats with bizarre names, a loving dog that looked after daughter number two, and a relatively normal suburban life, while he worked at building electronic devices in the rarified academic environment of Stanford University. It had been at the end of a long evening of wine drinking and pot smoking that he had convinced me that refusing the government tax money was a good way to express our resistance. Unlike many men his age, he had been exempted from the draft because of marriage and family, and now he wanted to make his political contribution. So far, so good. I went along with it because I had no reason not to. I continued to feel the love for him that I had so dramatically fallen into years ago, and I was moved by his impassioned voice. He was emphatically clear about a number of things in those days: the visionary power of science, passive resistance to war, the worthiness of Miles Davis and Buddy Holly, the hatefulness of Richard Nixon, and the delightful brain enhancing qualities of marijuana.

Life was comfortable overall, with convivial dinner parties on weekends, school camping trips, two cars, and a good stereo. While he gave his all to his research job at Stanford, I tried to become a housewife. Raised by a maverick mother, I never imagined my life this way, but instead I had dreams of becoming an interpreter, or pontificating in a courtroom far away from bake sales and carpools. Middle-class trappings abounded: symphony tickets, a Cuisinart, a small supply of evening clothes, organic foods, and our kids in private school, albeit an "alternative" one. I threw myself into cooking and became really good at it, making generous sprawling meals for my friends, and we all sat around the dinner table late into the night declaiming the war, right-wing politicians, and the extravagant price of good wine.

Jack and I didn't join the activists who hit the streets, risking safety and comfort, carrying scantily clad babies with tangled hair and smudged faces and colorful creative signs that spoke of the outrage. On quiet nights, we watched in shock as the broadcasting networks rolled out story after story of the carnage in Southeast Asia and the police brutality in America. We learned words we'd never heard before: napalm, Na Trang, Agent Orange, Da Nang . . . We managed to show up at a few marches in San Francisco with the girls, feeling proud of ourselves, but we never really committed to the cause. Our social lives, his work, our children's school schedules, vacations in Hawaii and Mexico—these kept us busy. I had a sneaking feeling that we were morally lazy, though I rarely admitted it. I lived with a man convinced of his own righteousness, after all; it was in his genes apparently, and he never seemed to have any doubt. I stuffed my misgivings the same way I had done with my mother, intent on not making waves or causing a stir, and I tried to push the doubts away.

I had been born into a family where much of our history was concealed. My grandmother, Ellen McCarter from Rumson, New Jersey, due to arrive on our doorstep soon, had been raised in a world where politics, drinking disorders, diseases, and marital problems were rarely aired in public. She had been a great beauty with perfectly round dark eyes and a perky little mouth, and she had a reputation for being a great storyteller after a few cocktails. It was the Irish in her, I guess. She rarely touched on anything dark or unattractive, and when the conversation turned to politics, finance, or war, she always deferred to the gentlemen in suits at her table. I had the impression that she trusted all who took care of her: the capitalist system, her accountant, her housekeeper, and the government. The whole wonderful system kept her in furs and sapphires, and she was certainly not disposed to object to the status quo. She played by society's rules.

When my mother, Madeleine, hastily decided to enlist in the WAVES at the end of the World War II, my grandmother was consumed with nationalistic pride, proclaiming her young daughter a true patriot at the bridge table. Or so the story goes. This was a time of growing patriotism and nostalgia throughout the country, and it never occurred to her that her daughter Madeleine had flown no further than Corpus Christi, Texas, motivated only by the desire to find a handsome young officer in uniform to seduce.

When my grandmother, Ellen, was finally delivered in a long black Cadillac to our little redwood home on the hill, we were prepared. Daunted by the stern message inherent in the government's proclamation, I had cleverly camouflaged the signs with a couple of art posters from the San Francisco Museum of Modern Art. Dressed in my best flowered Indian tunic and doing my best not to feel shy about her enormous limo out front, I served her iced tea with mint and lemon and homemade cookies. She sat in our wood-paneled living room in Redwood City with her perfectly coiffed gray hair, red lipstick, and pearls about her wrinkled neck, swirls of cigarette smoke rising from her dainty hand, and Jack and I "rose to the occasion," showing off our daughters and our quaint little house and garden—all as though there were no war, no jailed protestors, no trouble with the government, no fractured society—only the preciousness of our little family. About a month following this sweet domestic scene, we capitulated and paid our debt to the federal government, and the infamous signs were removed.

Vietnam raged on far away, and we continued to live protected lives, but I remember feeling this pocket of dingy guilt about our country's dishonesty in Vietnam. I learned how to make margaritas and thought I could forget all the darkness that surrounded us after sampling a few cocktails. Was this queasy feeling of mine connected to that line that had been crossed back in the sixties in America when innocence and hopefulness morphed into terror, our leaders were assassinated, and we couldn't find any answers? As the country soon came to know a perpetual mourning and pessimism, conversations around our safe little dinner table began to change, and I decided to go back to college and ultimately turn inward to look for some understanding.

Jack and I devoured all the war films that came to movie theaters then: *Platoon*, *The Deer Hunter*, and, of course, *Apocalypse Now*, all of which dramatized the destruction of body

and psyche of our young American men who were just following orders as they ravaged and burned Vietnam's landscape.
Later, in graduate school, when I came upon Joseph Conrad's
Heart of Darkness, on which *Apolcalypse (Apocalypse the correct
spelling) Now* was loosely based, I learned another dark and
mind-bending truth that drew my mind back to the horrors
of the Vietnam War that still lurked in my memory.

The novel tells of a long and frightening voyage on water
into literal and psychic darkness; Conrad wrote the book to
purge the savagery he had witnessed in the Belgian Congo
years earlier, as men from imperialist Western nations committed unspeakable acts out of greed for ivory. Conrad's alter
ego is named Marlow, and he narrates the journey through
a chaotic jungle where he has been commissioned to lead an
expedition into Congo territory to retrieve an ivory kingpin
named Kurtz who has gone quite mad. As the journey on
water progresses, we see the alien jungle landscape and the
white interloper filled with fear; we are carried by Conrad's
trustworthy voice and experience the events through his eyes.
We believe the whole story: the terror and disillusionment
of white imperialists, the mute fear and rage of the natives,
and the chaos of navigating the labyrinth of the dense jungle.
Time melts in this novel, and anxiety builds gradually as
Marlow's boat gets closer and closer to Kurtz's outpost where
human skulls are displayed on a series of poles as trophies.

When I first read the novel, I thought I understood
something profound about human beings: greed and cruelty
and ignorance are inevitable pieces of being human and they
lead to deep suffering. The continent of Africa was awash in
slave and ivory trade during the 1700 and 1800s, staining
the land with blood and suffocating any resistance, and this
short novel is a testament to one writer's courage in telling
the truth. Conrad's book, though slim, is epic. It traces man's

inner and outer journey and reminds us that as we move forward into the dark places, we inevitably encounter our greed, confusion, and terror, in addition to our own humanity, and it also suggests that the attainment of the goal rarely brings resolution. When Marlow finally comes upon the pathological fake demigod Mr. Kurtz at the Inner Station, he feels neither relief nor surprise. The dying Kurtz mumbles, "The horror, the horror!" as Marlow's men carry him back to the boat and a return to the civilization that he will never join. Later Marlow will lie when he meets Kurtz's "Intended" (fiancée) in Europe, who begs to know that his last words were of her. Why does he lie? Perhaps because there are things about life in the darkness that we cannot communicate to those who choose to live in the light. Marlow feels his own darkened heart, but he resorts to civility, which is far more comfortable than the truth, and then he goes on his way so he may begin to mend his wounds far away from the darkness he has found in the human heart.

Hanoi Streets

Life in Hanoi in the twenty-first century is a far cry from the smoke-filled landscape of war during the 1970s. Economic prosperity of sorts has arrived, and with it, cars and motorbikes, cell phones, girls in tight pants and bright makeup, and more cars and motorbikes. Early on in my Hanoi visit, I had a chance to see what my young guide put forth as an authentic part of the city, the "old quarter," where all the streets were named for the different kinds of goods that had been peddled there long ago: silk, cotton, bronze, drums, silver, paper, and wood. Quaint, old . . . good, I thought. After making myself race behind Duang across a few scary crowded roundabouts with cars whirring by on all sides, I began to feel that there was little of the antique to be found in this city many call the "French capital of the East." He then handed me over to a scrawny but strong looking older man who would carry me in his cyclo on a journey through the old zone in what I imagined would be dignified and instructive experience. I was nervous about having no language skills and feeling cut off, and also self-conscious that, as a somewhat hefty Westerner, I might cause this older man physical strain. Perhaps I had forgotten that Westerners are rarely fluent in the Asian languages, and that these tiny men who haul the large visitors around in their little half-bicycles have been making a living doing this for a very long time.

Off we went into the maze of the old quarter. The little streets were painfully narrow, and I craned my neck to be able to catch the quaint names of the streets (Cotton, Silk, Leather) displayed both in Vietnamese and in English, but to no avail. Surrounding us on both sides were masses of people on motorbikes and bicycles, in cars and on foot. It felt as though we were on a moving motorway stuck in place while still being pushed along. The honking and screeching was deafening, and the exhaust from the trucks and cars left a bitter taste on my tongue. Our little buggy moved haltingly, it seemed, while motorbikes skillfully threaded their way through the masses. Instead of being able to escape my carriage once in a while and take pictures of the colorful storefronts, I got a dizzying blur of faces and helmets in passing. I caught sight of sparkling costumes in one window, then shops with bold political posters, and the fish mongers, and then herbal medicine shops with giant squat burlap bags out front. Musty mushroom smells, tingling herbal perfumes. On the back of many speeding bicycles were huge piles of mangoes and bananas flashing green and yellow. Everything seemed to move straight up from the street, as all the slender buildings formed a series of small canyons. This was a vertical universe. I wanted to stop and look at the giant eels swimming in buckets and the political posters and the herbs and the quaint straw hats, but I didn't quite know how to communicate this to my trusty driver, and so the opportunity vanished.

As we rolled through the tiny congested streets where Hanoians did their shopping and lived their lives, I recalled walking the streets of Shanghai in the late nineties, feeling as though I were being swallowed by the density of city people moving separately through their lives, always smoking and toting odd plastic bags, staring at the white woman with mistrust or indifference. I was alien to them then, and I am now, I think. The shift in perspective had felt unnerving and humbling as it did now, and it made me feel a lot less inquisitive about the smelly and exotic show that unfolded in front of me. Here in my little cyclo, I felt a similar version of the claustrophobia and disconnection I had felt on Shanghai streets. These feelings were all too familiar to me, conjuring my childhood fears when I had to ride a crowded sweaty bus in Rome and couldn't breathe, or the many times I'd felt I lost contact with my body and disappeared in the company of those I lived with.

When my driver, who never broke a sweat in our hourlong journey, delivered me back to the glistening white Metropole Hotel, I felt relieved. I turned away then from the gritty indifferent streets and greeted the concierge in his little pill box hat and cream-colored uniform who spoke to me warmly in his best French. Now I'd let go of the terrified self who felt alien and vulnerable, leave behind the street's mysteries, and enter the nostalgic perfumed stage set of the French colonial world. My search for the authentic would have to continue another time.

Halong's Waters

Many hours north of Hanoi is a remarkable place called Halong Bay, an ancient grouping of limestone islets just a short boat ride from the unremarkable-looking harbor town of Halong. Almost two thousand of these tiny islands poke up out of the dark waters, some of them hollow, others with giant dripping caves. I joined a group of other foreign travelers to board a boat named the *Jasmine Junk* for a cruise through the maze that is Halong. On this polished little vessel, we glided off into the seascape for two nights and a day to sail in and around the mysterious rock formations. The weather was gray and cloudy and stayed that way for the duration, disappointing most of my companions who wished for a sea sparkling in sunlight. Having grown up in the fog-shrouded city of San Francisco, nicknamed by one local writer, "the cool gray city of love," I felt comforted in this moment by the gray climate. With gray, we are in the uncertain middle ground in the world of color; it spells mystery to me, and this mystery allows my imagination to get up and dance.

The history of Halong is ancient. I could feel it. Standing at the prow of the *Jasmine Junk* and looking forward into the layers of water, rock, and mist, I felt I was journeying back in time to some mythic place of high adventure on a grand sailing ship. I thought of the story of brave Odysseus, the Homeric hero who spent much of his life traveling on the sea, enduring many tests of character so that he might return to Ithaka and Penelope, his beloved wife. From island to island he had sailed, seduced by women, manipulated by both the gods and the men around him, and led astray by his own ignorant sense of self, but always under the protective watch of the goddess Athena who was determined to get him home. If I had a guide and protector on my world travels, it would have to have been my grandmother Dimond, whose love for me and zest for adventure in the world had colored my young life.

The next morning, we were ushered into tiny little rowboats to take a floating journey to see a few local fishing villages. When we arrived at the first one, I suddenly became aware of a living, breathing Vietnam, one I hadn't touched in the stage-set worlds of Hoi An, Hue, or Hanoi. The families in this community lived on little houseboats complete with potted flowers and an occasional scruffy cat or dog on their decks. Their brightly painted doors and windows were open to the outside; We peered in as we glided by, at the women sewing or tending children, and the men working on fishing nets or dozing quietly in chairs off to the side. These houseboats were trimmed in freshly painted bright greens, blues, and reds that popped out in the blurry gray mist. This little community seemed lonely to me, so far from the world of commerce and movement, but as I looked closer, I saw contentment in the dailiness of their lives. They carried their bodies with ease, they were paying close attention to their work, and yes, they smiled.

There are over 1600 people who live and work in these floating villages, and they survive through fishing and various kinds of marine aquaculture, since the bay is rich in hundreds of species of fish and mollusks. We saw young boys out in simple fishing boats, laughing and working at the same time, their slippery little bodies brown with exposure to the sun. They seemed to find our fleet of small rowboats loaded with large white people amusing. There was much smiling and waving at our pointed cameras. We heard few sounds; the silence was heavy about us. A little giggle from a fisher-boy from time to time, the slapping of oars on water (*plap, plap, plap . . . shhhhhhhh*), a lonely bird cry. We floated quietly for an hour or more, and watched these people of the sea who, like prehistoric sea turtles that for centuries have crawled from the ocean to particular beaches in the world to lay their eggs in the sand and perpetuate their survival, seem to work with some unspoken ancient plan to maintain the lives of their families.

I felt wistful and resistant to leaving this perfectly peaccful place, as our little boats eventually turned themselves around later and headed for our sparkling junk floating in the distance. Images of this impermanent and textured experience remained in my head even as I sat down for a drink with some of my fellow travelers later that evening. Dark descended on our boat swaying a little in the mist, and we talked on into the evening over good food and wine in the wood-paneled dining room, energized by the camaraderie and the pleasure of hearing the English language spilling forth at will. When I examined my photographs of this mysterious landscape some months later, I recalled the very simple pleasure of moving through space on a boat in gray waters where people's lives unfolded quietly, and the visitor was invited to see how connected we humans are as we try to create our own lives of peace, wellbeing, and understanding.

In the gray fog of Halong Bay, I think I understood that even though the tide of change is unavoidable, and the need to put historical memories in their proper place and move on is of value, some very old ways of taking care of life endure in Vietnam as well as elsewhere in Asia. I just needed to slow down, not think too much, and pay close attention to the mystery.

Nine: The Shadow of Death in Cambodia

The Heat and the Bones

As Phe Try slowly began to tell his and his country's story in the car on the way to the Killing Fields, the dusty Phnom Penh streets blurring by in a sticky heat outside, my mind found the anchor it needed to get its bearings. It was January of 2013, and I was on my second pilgrimage to Cambodia, trying to get a little closer to understanding this country's burden of suffering. What came into focus as I struggled to breathe through the heat was: *This man lived through the horror to tell his story.*

As a child he'd nearly starved to death in a Khmer Rouge labor camp, a young boy of eight whose family members disappeared and were later exterminated. He told the tale with little punctuation or emphasis, moving toward the point in the narrative where he eventually could attend school to learn English and finally find work as a travel guide. As he grew up, he took on a military career whose rules and order helped him erase some of the deep grief for a while. But in the end, it couldn't sustain him emotionally, and he finally chose work that would bring him in contact with many non-Cambodians and allow him to hold the losses and speak the truth about what had happened.

I remember the sunlight was so white that it hurt my eyes as we walked among the burial holes at the Killing Fields. Here many thousands of "untrainable" Cambodians—men, women, and young ones who couldn't be transformed into good communists—were executed and dumped by the Khmer Rouge. There must have been fifteen different large holes in the earth that we stood and stared at as we both reflected on—or in Phe Try's case, *remembered*—the massacre. A few human bones rested on the dry ground as grim symbols of what this place was about. Here and there were pieces of children's torn clothing. I paused at each mass grave and tried to imagine what had transpired—*but how could I possibly imagine?*

I remembered the images I had seen long ago in news reports of the child soldiers armed with guns larger than they were, and the stories of the tiny babies ripped from their parents' arms. I shook my head and asked Try, "How can humankind turn on itself like this?" He must have taken my question as rhetorical. Ignoring my query, he continued his gentle, matter-of-fact telling of the reign of terror: the eradication of all who were educated or unproductive, the training of children to kill, and the forced labor camps like the one where he had been imprisoned at seven and from which he had escaped alone at the end of it all. Larger philosophical questions clearly meant little to Try, as they could not help him heal; they belonged instead in wood-paneled classrooms and offices of academia rather than this landscape where people had struggled to survive. I heard no emotion in his voice, just the steady, soft-spoken account of a starving young boy who survived on bowls of watery porridge and never knew from one day to the next if he would ever see loved ones again or have his freedom.

"We were fed only once a day . . . a small bowl of water with just few grains of rice in it . . . that's all. The worst time was the nighttime, when we had to sleep in rags with hunger pains that kept us awake." Try's gentle brown eyes stared off into the bright light beyond me.

As a tour guide, Try has revisited these fields and the S-21 prison day after day and intoned his country's horrific story. I assumed that he saw this job as a sacred duty; his soft forty-something brown face was proud, but his gait was gimpy and disjointed, and his left leg twitched erratically whenever he was still and seated, the trauma of those early wounds showing up in his body.

Around we walked in the breathless morning sun until we reached a tall cylindrical shrine-like building made of glass. I entered here, after leaving a small bunch of white flowers and lighting a stick of incense, and began to walk in a circle around the display of thousands of skulls, legs, arms, and pelvis bones neatly placed on dusty, untended shelves which rose to the sky almost twenty feet high. There weren't many people visiting the shrine that morning, and I was grateful for the chance to be a solitary witness of the relics. The skulls gripped my attention the most—they came in all sizes, dusty tan, creamy and smooth, bleached and parched . . . all with gaping dark eye sockets. I felt the inclination to cup my hand around the back of a skull, to feel its per-fect rounded form, to remember there was once a human consciousness inside. What that mind had witnessed forty years ago, I could never imagine: a child soldier swinging an AK-47 and screaming orders hysterically, men and women everywhere, birdlike in their thinness, flattened out on the ground, and oozing blood, bodies crushed, limbs scattered, and the bleeding everywhere. These bones, formed from the earth, made me conscious of my own perfect skeleton of 206 bones, the very same form as those I was now staring at.

When I visit places of death on my travels, it often brings to mind two of my literary heroes who knew death well: Homer and Dante. These men were driven to explore and reflect on the Underworld in order to understand man's humanity. As Odysseus wanders among the shades in Hades, and Dante travels through the circles of hell in the *Inferno*, they rejoin characters from their lives and learn of their suffering; they cast away judgment and come to accept their own vulnerability and humanity. Epic thinkers like Homer and Dante believed that the hero must find a shared humanity in order to gain what he deeply loved and cherished: family, home, country. When we take a good look at the realm of the dead, we see the human family we belong to and come to understand we're just other beings in the long procession of life, that journey of flesh-covered skeletons moving through their days until the final letting go. I noticed there were no labels for these bones lying on the shelves before me. There probably hadn't been enough time or manpower, I thought, just too many bodies to record them all, too much grief and loss. The people who needed to know the names of the dead might have been told, or not, but this was not my business. What I did know was that these Cambodians whose bodies had been excavated from the mass graves were my relatives in the larger human family—I understood this in a profound way as I stared at their remains, even though their skin had been a warm caramel brown and their Khmer language an ancient tongue that sounded like rippling soft music. My own living, breathing body felt weak and transparent as if it were losing form, and an aching sadness like the worst headache of my life pushed down on me from above. At last, through the oppressive heat, I walked away from these souls and rejoined my guide.

Eventually I didn't feel the heat so much as a big wall but rather as something swampy that I waded through, as Try and I continued our march together through the fields. I veered toward what small patches of shade were available and tried to objectify my discomfort: noticing my leather watchband becoming an oily dark color on my damp wrist, tracking the lines of sweat running down my back and from my forehead into my eyes. I followed his story of Cambodia's suffering as I walked, my thick eyeliner becoming muddy and stinging my tired eyes. *This is just heat,* I said to myself when I wasn't hating it; suffering followed, as my meditation teachers had often reminded me, when I remained attached to my aversion. Somewhere inside the murkiness of my mind and my numbing sense of despair, I sensed I was losing considerable body mass from all the sweat dripping from my limbs. And we marched on. . . .

As Try continued to describe the emaciated lifeless bodies tossed by the hundreds into the pits after execution, I began to feel ashamed of being preoccupied with my own overheated body that walked not so mindfully over the dusty remains of thousands. Before long, the midday Phnom Penh heat became a breathless container that literally held the two of us and carried us forward as though in a dream until the moment we finally found our local driver, who welcomed us into the dusty red air-conditioned car that would take us to our next stop.

S-21

Later the same day, we visited Tuol Sleng prison, also known as S-21, the infamous site in Phnom Penh where close to 14,000 people were incarcerated and tortured in the late 1970s. It is now called Tuol Sleng Genocide Museum, but it had once been a simple high school before the Khmer Rouge. As I walked through the grimy dark interior, I tried to imagine all the children sitting attentively in classrooms with lined notebooks and chewed off pencils, or those joyously kicking a football in the yard, on the brink of the rest of their lives. Room after room, the place was filled with riveting old photographs and instruments of torture, such as big heavy chains on the stone floors that bound people in place. Inside this building, it was deep-in-the-bones cold, the hot steaminess of outdoors now far away. Try walked unevenly beside me and remained silent; there was much to look at on the walls, documents to read, faces to study. I read all the information with my hand on my heart. I was telling Try about the book I had been reading at home before my trip—*The Lost Executioner*, which described the search for the last surviving S-21 commandant, a mysterious character named Duch—when I came upon a striking black-and-white photograph of this very man most historians called the most notorious of the Khmer Rouge murderers. This faded print showed an inscrutable man with a drawn face and paranoid eyes. Something about it made real the unspeakable acts I had learned of, sending a ripple of cold through my body.

During our little tour, I saw that the Khmer Rouge had chosen to document most of the people they had exterminated with photographs. I had always thought of photography as a respectful capturing of people and place, the creation of art to preserve memory and character, but what I saw here in this dingy gallery at the old prison showed no regard for Cambodian life. It was simply a means of keeping track of the numbers captured and killed. I felt wobbly on my feet as I looked at the large dark wall of haggard faces; I was grateful for these faces that seemed to reach out to me with their sunken eyes. We were now frozen in time, and these sad faces reminded me of what happened here, inviting me in with their eyes, those windows to their souls. I paused a while in front of these portraits and felt my own heart beating away deep inside; if I remained long enough, if time could somehow melt away and bring us together, I was sure I'd hear their voices asking gently for my attention.

Of the many thousands of prisoners incarcerated here, only seven were spared in the end, because they were artists. Their creative lives made reprieve possible. Lice were combed from their hair, they were cleaned up, given solid food (real rice as opposed to broth with a few grains floating in it) and an unshackled place to sleep, and were then commissioned to paint and sculpt portraits of Pol Pot. And they were allowed to live. One of these men, named Bou Meng, still lives in Phnom Penh, and on some days you can find this fragile gentleman peddling his small memoir at a table by the entrance to the museum. He spent the better part of his post-prison life trying to secure an admission of responsibility for his wife's execution, eventually confronting the commandant Duch himself. Even though he possessed an artist's heart and mind, he was unable to forgive this man who confessed to the murder. The stories of these artists reminded me of a handful of Jewish women prisoners at Auschwitz who were musicians and escaped extermination because they could play sublime Beethoven Quartets for the German High Command. This freedom came at a horrific price, but their story was ultimately transformed into an important movie by Arthur Miller in 1980 called *Playing for Time*.

Is it possible that deep in the psyche of the deranged captor there are tender places that can respond to the unfolding of beauty? When I contemplate cruel, unspeakable suffering in places like Auschwitz, Rwanda, Vietnam, Afghanistan, South Africa, and even the dark history of our own South, I tell myself that it must be so. The phenomenal creation that is the human mind/heart holds a mysterious connection to beauty deep inside. It is called "spirit," and it is transcendent, creating a bridge for man between the sane and the insane.

Cambodia lost close to an entire generation during the reign of terror that lasted barely four years—over one million gone. Today people over forty are small in number, and they continue to carry their people's loss in their bones. This country is a nation of young people, I noticed, who struggle in a state whose government is as depleted and broken as their elders had been; they work harder than we in the West can imagine to get out from under the cloud of economic injustice and the holocaust of forty years ago. Their dark history lingers still. The saffron-robed monks who walk the poor streets each day with their begging bowls remind Cambodians that human compassion is possible, but the lines of grief on most people's faces—restaurant workers, tuk-tuk drivers, crippled booksellers on the streets, tour guides and souvenir peddlers—remind those of us who visit that the layers of grief in this land are deep.

A Mother Returns

Very early the morning following our visit to the prison, I woke suddenly from a dream so vivid that I thought I had just come from the bedside of my dying mother, now gone over twenty years. A woman who had suffered deeply, who lost her faith in life, she died alone in a San Francisco hospital with a bloated liver, seized up lungs, and an abiding terror. I had tried to get to her bedside, traveling on two planes across various states, but I missed my chance to hold her hand before she died. In my Phnom Penh dream, I was entering a lovely bedroom in my grandmother's old house—a place where I had spent so many comforting years. My mother reclined on pillows, right on the edge of dying, looking more radiant and beautiful than she had most of her life; her face with the dramatic high forehead was luminous, and although she was entirely bald and pale white, her velvet brown eyes were still strong. I could almost smell the lavender lotion she loved so, but no, that was part of the time when she lived. She was now fading away, skeletal and serene. On the verge of dying, she stared at me with loving awareness, as though she were about to say these words: "I love you, Mag." We both smiled at one another—although no words were spoken that I can remember—but the moment stretched out beautifully. Each of us knew exactly where we were, and it felt so good to be in each other's company.

Now, in my air-conditioned hotel room on this humid morning, my body felt both chilled and calm as I awoke and pondered the gift of this dream. It was as though my sleep that night had been visited by a procession of Cambodian skulls and bones and floating spirits who had never found their rest on earth, and they had brought my dying mother back to me so she and I could finally find some peace. I felt gratitude's warmth deep in my body, and in my mind an unsettling irony that it was in *this very country*, where many thousands of citizens fought with every fiber of their being to survive war and torture, that my confused and heartsick mother, who cared so little for her life that she slowly killed herself, finally came back to me.

My mother died alone in a hospital room in San Francisco in the middle of the night. The date was December 1, 1991. As I traveled to arrive at her bedside from my home in New Mexico, over a thousand miles away, I repeated stubbornly to myself: *I must reach her.*

She will see me now, will know me in the end, I kept promising myself. There was one phone call with a hospital doctor midway through my journey where he told me that she was coming out of the ICU and showed signs of improvement. I remember I said to him, "Please tell her I am coming. It's important that she know." I spent a restless night in a hotel before taking another plane to San Francisco. Then there was a second call when I was changing planes in Phoenix; I was on my way, I said as I stood at the airport payphone. But Mom's sister-in-law's flat voice on the other end of the phone told me she was dead.

"She died at two in the morning in the hospital," she said flatly, and I thought, *She died in the dark and alone.*

I stood there absolutely still in that unfamiliar airport on Thanksgiving weekend, where masses of travelers hurried onward, and I felt all the sounds around me move through my body: little children's pleading voices, twangy PA announcements, people talking fretfully as they marched, and the relentless clacking of roller bags on concrete. I put the phone down empty-hearted. My breathing was so shallow I could hardly find it; my mind flailed about in confusion, not understanding. How do you understand that your mother, who gave you life, is gone for good? It felt as though my physical body were disappearing in all the confusion. I stood still for a while, rooted in place, and waited for something to come, tears or grief, some kind of plan, something, but there was nothing. Then I remembered something deeply familiar from my years of living with her. It was her voice saying, "Dearie, when things get really tough, just find the nearest bar and order a drink, and then everything will get better!" Yes. I would honor her passing through her own method of choice. I would feel her closer to me then, and not have to imagine her lying cold and frightened in the dark.

I shouldered my heavy purse and dragged my carryon bag down a few nondescript corridors lined with bookstores, coffee shops, and anonymous restrooms, until I came to the Sunshine Grill with its huge blaring television, mirrored backdrop, and weary-looking customers. I plopped myself on a barstool and ordered my mother's favorite daytime drink. Staring into my very red Bloody Mary, I felt a wave of chaotic sensations: memories of her whipping up her own well-known Bloody Marys, so strong they looked pink and not red; thoughts of the tragic Mary Queen of Scots who, I thought in my fuzzy imagination, was the drink's namesake; remembering too my mother's fascination with English history, her love affair with abstract art, and her attachment to Chanel No. 5. Strange to call a drink "bloody"—or was it, I mused as I looked into my spicy red cocktail with the perky celery stalk, hearing a faint echo of her words, "You bloody well need to *rise to the occasion*, Maggie, now is not the time to tell me about your feelings. . . ." *Yes, Mom, I do need to rise to the occasion now of all times, but the thing is: I don't know how.*

How remarkable this blood of ours is, this salty crimson fluid that is an invisible messenger running through our veins, keeping us alive until the journey ends; the stuff painfully extracted from our arms so the doctors can understand more about our bodies and help us heal; that runs through our purple ropey "old lady" veins that become bumpy and dark as we age. The dark red fluid that, in one of my most frightening memories, spattered the walls of my mother's pretty pink bathroom in San Francisco just a year before her death.

Back in California for a visit, my partner Charlie and I had joined my mother for dinner with some visiting friends. She had left the restaurant early, claiming she felt unwell. When we returned to her apartment, we were greeted with great wailing and hand wringing on the part of her house-keeper, Lena. Mom had retreated to the bathroom as soon as she arrived home, and this gentle Filipino woman had found her collapsed over the edge of the bathtub, blood spewing from her stomach that she had so relentlessly poisoned, splattering the lovely pink walls, the towels, and the white bathtub. Charlie loved to take charge of emergencies, and so he held me back from witnessing the horror scene of dark clotted blood on towels and tub, on the pink walls and fuzzy bedroom slippers, the sour, rank smell hanging in the air. Her body had spoken its truth, I knew this at the time. It was bleeding away its life. I didn't want to see her this way and so accepted Charlie's intervention—yet in my head, I could visualize the horrors unfolding in the bathroom, as my weakened mother was carried off to her soft bed and the mopping of the tub and floor began.

From the time I was a little girl, I had watched my mother consume inhuman amounts of alcohol, but it was a long time before I could admit to myself that she was slowly killing herself. As she aged, she consistently ignored all medical warnings that came to her, changing doctors as often as she was given ominous news. A lot of years dragged on—the liver is a mighty and stubborn organ—but as she became paler, her stomach more bloated, her eyes showed me her fear of dying, all wide and nervous and bloodshot. The liver had begun to rot, now beyond rescuing, and soon there would be no more martinis or brandies or cigarettes. No more.

Mom had always loved a pink-and-red landscape, like the one she finally collapsed in. Back in the fifties, when I was nine years old, she had her classic MG painted a special rich pink; she was convinced it was the only pink classic MG with red upholstery in all of San Francisco! I remember riding in the tiny back compartment as a kid to and from school and feeling proud to be driven around in such a brazen little car. And then the red and the pink showed up in that gritty abstract painting of hers that now hangs in my house by the beach, heavy with layered paint and memories of her love of color. She often wore pink nightgowns, painted her toenails pink, and had her dresser drawer lined with rosy flowered paper, but in the end, she died in a sterile room away from pink walls, porcelain ornaments, and bright paintings; and I never knew whether she went peacefully.

I'm pretty sure that she did not let go of life peacefully. She had a Dylan Thomas kind of mind, she and her third husband, Peter, who had died just three years before after a lifetime of abuse. "Do not go gentle into that dark night. . . ." There was nothing gentle about the way those two had cared for themselves. I wasn't rushing to her bedside on Thanksgiving weekend to ask her to choose life over death for my children who loved her, for herself, or for the love I silently carried for her. I knew that it was too late for the "staying alive" conversation. She had long ago made her choice against life. Even so, I had wanted her to know I was going to show up, sit with her through the night, even hold her hand, and tell her I loved her. It seemed like the least I could do, because, you see, there was just a small chance that she had taken that kind of loving care of me during some dark nights when I was little, a time too far away for me to remember anymore. Sadly, I would never know whether the doctor on the phone took seriously my plea to tell her that I was coming.

A few weeks later, I found a way to make some peace with her, as I brought her ashes home in a pink (yes, pink!) plastic bag from the Neptune Society, and placed them gently on the coffee table in my small apartment. Some ritual was called for, but what would that look like? I didn't know. She certainly had never taught me. I wanted to run my fingers through her pebbly ashes, which I imagined would feel warm like beach sand, to dig in and touch what remained of her, and see if there were any remnants of the gold wedding band she had refused to give up. Then a little know-it-all voice whispered: No, no, not that. So instead I quietly sent love to her, remembering some of the sweet moments of our life together: my tenth birthday in the snowy mountains at Tahoe, our visits to feed the wild cats at the Coliseum in Rome, how much fun it was to dance around the dining room to Dixieland records pretending we were wild women. Then I wished her safe passage; she needed that, I figured. She stayed in the room with me for quite a while, filling up the living room with her restlessness and faded perfume. It was cocktail time, after all.

Perhaps I had been afraid that feeling her grit and ashes on my hands would force me to see she was nothing any-more—just dust—and that would deepen the hollow place in my chest. Tears would finally come, and I'd have a hard time sealing the urn correctly so she could be transported home to New York to be buried beside her mother in the family plot on Long Island. That December evening was so quiet and gentle, so perfect. I finally lit a cigarette in her honor and toasted her with a generous glass of Chardonnay, as the sky beyond the Golden Gate Bridge softened into a beautiful pink sunset that would have made her very happy.

Forgiveness and Letting Go

On some level I did make peace with my mother, not only on that tranquil December afternoon spent with her ashes, but also through all the years since 1991 when, as a struggling Buddhist, I practiced forgiveness for myself, for her, and for others. Forgiveness and letting go were foreign to me when I stood at her gravesite on Long Island, waiting to see her ashes placed in the ground. All I could think or feel then was bleak despair that she had never known how or wanted to be my mother, that she had chosen other people and other pursuits instead of me. My heart remained closed in that frigid landscape as the rest of the family pretended to be in mourning for this beautiful black sheep member of the family. Peace would come to me later, but of course I didn't know it then.

Since my two journeys to Cambodia, I have often wondered just how those who survive terror make peace with the epic loss of their people. How are forgiveness and reconciliation possible? In America, we are conditioned by the narrative of the individual, and we are driven to find closure *for just ourselves* so that we may function with our sadness buried deep inside. It is all very personal. There are so many places on this planet where the citizens don't have this luxury, countries like South Africa, Vietnam, Burma, India, Rwanda, China, Nicaragua—just to mention some—where history has dealt the people horrific, inhuman suffering and loss, and all that can be done in the end is to embrace the whole dark mess and continue to move forward with an open forgiving heart and an honest voice.

I have a friend who is a Cambodian poet. His name is Sam Oeur. He lived through the Killing Fields, camouflaging his education and his status as best he could so his family could survive. Despite playing by the rules, he saw his twin babies ripped out of their mother's arms and strangled before his eyes. And that is not all the horror that he saw. He is a frail eighty years old now, living a simple life with his family in America as he continues to write poetry; he still carries the trauma inside. Sam practiced as a Buddhist monk for many years in middle age and attempted to find equanimity and ease, and yet he was always an advocate for his people. He found that writing poetry was the only way to endure his and his country's suffering. He writes in Khmer, with its beautiful singsong cadence and nervous rhythm, and chants his verses to those who want to listen, telling his story of his life and his nation's life torn apart. In his first published book, *Sacred Vows*, he writes, "I'd rather be destitute than abandon my vows." His vows are to live his life dedicated to the Buddha's teachings of wisdom and compassion, and to never give up on telling the story of his country. "I try to survive for my nation," he says.

This is how I imagine most people recover from trauma: they speak the truths of exile and torture, even when they feel it's impossible to do so; they take care of their precious bodies; and through the truth-telling, they cultivate kindness and forgiveness, so that all those who have no way of knowing will see that the human spirit is a mighty thing in the darkness. The spirit can and does rise above horrors. An Afghani woman named Malalai Joya, who has lived through unspeakable dangers in her own country defending women's rights, reportedly said this about the fearless life: "You can destroy the flowers, but you can never stop the spring." I can imagine my friend Sam saying those very words.

I have never suffered in the ways these people have, never seen the fabric of my culture ripped apart and my loved ones executed, but I've always believed that in order to build a conscious and good life, I had to tell the truth. I had to tell my mother I knew our family was falling apart; I had to tell my children I had deceived them many times; I had to tell my husband I had betrayed him for another; I had to tell myself I carried as many flaws and scary ghosts as my mother, who denied her alcoholism and died because of it.

If my mother's death and the brave lives of my two Cambodian comrades taught me anything, it is that you may well die from not telling the truth.

Ten: Coming Home
to San Francisco

How are we shaped by all the places in which we have lived and traveled? Sometimes I imagine my answer as a series of puzzle pieces that can be fit together carefully to create a cohesive whole, and other times I think the whole thing is a composition of random mosaic fragments. I've looked at my life stories through a kaleidoscope, all the colorful luminous pieces drifting and sliding and coming together as a bright light shone through but failing to resemble linear narrative. This calls into question the subject of memory with its slippery and unreliable nature, and our ability to gather all the important pieces and translate them into a coherent life story. The piece of this puzzle that feels like the "through line" is San Francisco, my hometown. My home.

I wasn't born in San Francisco, but I have always felt I was a native, that I belonged. It was here that I found my first true friend at age three, grew up listening to foreign languages on the city's streets, rested securely in my grandmother's bed as sea air and foghorns comforted me, was introduced to modern art, opera, and proper table manners while carrying on a lengthy love affair with food. I gave birth here to my second child, and found drugs, sex, and rock 'n' roll in the late sixties. I left love behind and then found it again. I had my heart broken and tried a few honorable professions like teaching and making art. Throughout my childhood, I entered countless restaurants and learned about beautiful food from around the world and how to find the best steak on the menu. I may not have been born here, but I am *of this place*, and I have a feeling I will die here, as did my grandmother and mother. There is a comfort in that.

San Francisco shaped me with its unusual neighborhoods, the rolling hilly landscape falling down to the water, and the many restaurants where I learned to be a foodie. I have lived in many neighborhoods, slept in many houses, and eaten in hundreds of restaurants, but there are particular ones, rich with story, that rise now to the surface of my imperfect memory, that shine and dance before me. These are the ones: the places that anchor me in the past and cause me to reflect on the uncertain adventure of becoming an old lady.

Neighborhoods

Gritty North Beach

We moved to North Beach in 1954, around the time my mother divorced my father and began her search for a new mate. It was a colorful community in the northeast corner of the city, where the Italian immigrants had set up camp around 1860. Located between San Francisco's Fisherman's Wharf and a bustling produce district, both landscapes traditionally dominated by Italians, it was a natural place for the Italian fishermen from Genoa to claim as theirs when they immigrated in the 1800s. At its heart lay Washington Square, where old men and women sat on park benches spinning out their afternoons visiting, negotiating, laughing, and gossiping, their operatic language floating in the air along with the cigar smoke. In the "olden days," North Beach always felt more like a village than an urban neighborhood, and over time it became populated with many Italian restaurants, all cheap, many serving food family style at big long tables offering up a hospitable chaos. Dark little hole-in-the-wall smoky coffee houses cropped up everywhere, and as I walked home over gritty streets, the smell of bitter dark roast hung in the air along with the ever-present smell of sizzling hot garlic.

My mother loved this neighborhood because it was untidy, eccentric, bohemian, and it came alive at night, which suited her then. She sought adventure and drama. I liked it because it was so unlike the terribly quiet, clean neighborhood of Pacific Heights where very little seemed to happen, and it seemed like a foreign country. After Mom finished her studies at the California School of Fine Arts and began to reinvent herself as an abstract painter, our house on Green Street became a gathering place for her fellow artists, who came to spend long evenings in our living room over red wine and pasta as the candles flickered and wax dripped from the straw-covered Chianti bottles. Mom was now single, and she started to go out with the new men in her world: a pot-smoking clarinet player called Bill, a local band leader named Bob Scobey, and finally an out-of-work teacher called Raymond, whom she would eventually convince to marry her.

North Beach was filled then with poets and writers and artists—it was San Francisco's "left bank." These mavericks and visionaries gathered in the bars and coffee houses, gave readings, showed off their art, and pontificated about freedoms of all kinds and against anything that smacked of the mainstream. Everywhere you looked, people were smoking cigarettes and drinking espresso. The Beatnik movement was winding down by the late fifties, leaving behind an attitude of brash bohemian pride, some seedy bars open twenty hours a day, and a few edgy coffee houses that would be forever associated with the neighborhood, even after the pioneer of topless entertainment, Carol Doda with her fifty-inch breasts, brought sleaziness into the North Beach neighborhood in the form of guys in shiny dark suits and quasi-naked girls dancing in cages on top of flag poles.

We lived at 407 Green Street in a single-family square stucco house next to a lonely vacant lot, and I walked up a couple of steep hills to go to school at Garfield Elementary along with the Chinese, Italian, and Mexican kids. Our house was pretty plain on the outside, but inside the white walls were covered with enormous abstract paintings in wild colors. We had knocked a wall out between the living and dining rooms and left the rough beams so my mother could tack clippings, photographs, gallery announcements, and notes to the family right onto the wood. It wasn't a wall anymore, but an eye-catching installation. She worked for a while as a cocktail waitress at a club called the Tin Angel down by the waterfront, where local bands played Dixieland, and on other evenings she went out with her new friends while I stayed at home with a babysitter and frozen food in aluminum trays.

I walked alone in the neighborhood a lot, peering into coffee shops and the Co-Existence Bagel shop and the kooky vintage clothing store on Grant Avenue, and sometimes I hung around with Joe Greco, my best friend at Garfield School. He had brown skin and really dark eyes, and he spoke softly. We took picnics up to Coit Tower on Telegraph Hill, right above the school, and we sat among the eucalyptus trees and talked about who we wanted to be friends with, and about how we despised Miss Love, who kept us in constant fear during the week. We tucked ourselves into a safe place up there and watched the tourists and the hikers make the march up to the tower so they could catch the famous view of San Francisco Bay. Even today the smell of greasy dark red salami recalls the oversized sandwiches I used to buy at Molinari's—crusty sourdough bread, stacks of Provolone, tomato, and lettuce, peppery meat, and lots of mayo and mustard—and the camaraderie he and I enjoyed with each other.

Once my mother found her new husband, we ate dinner out a lot in the neighborhood. Italian restaurants were everywhere, but our favorite place was La Pantera on Grant Avenue, just a few blocks from our house, a dimly lit but boisterous place with red-checkered long tables, where we sat with others as giant steaming bowls of minestrone, pasta al pesto, and finally the greasy roast chicken or veal showed up on our tables. The wine was always in unmarked bottles, and the tangy sourdough bread came in tacky white plastic baskets. No one cared about finesse in those days when you got to savor all that great garlic in the pasta, the mountains of fresh-grated Parmesan, and a dinner that cost just four dollars. La Pantera was one of the most popular of the many Italian places in North Beach, because it was cheap and lively and made you feel like you were being welcomed to a foreign country for just a little while. It was here that Adlai Stevenson appeared when he was campaigning in California against Eisenhower for president in 1956. He ate dinner inside the restaurant with Mamma Luisa and then came outside to thank all the supporters gathered on Grant Avenue. My leftie mother adored Stevenson, though she always said he was too highbrow and intelligent to be elected president against a wartime hero like Ike. And she was right. But that magical night we were part of the cheering crowd and it was a beautiful summer evening, and Mr. Stevenson grabbed a rose from a bouquet and tossed it into the crowd along with his words of thanks for the city's support. My short little mother jumped up and caught it, as thrilled in the moment as if he had handed it to her personally with a big smile; she kept it for weeks in a water glass on the kitchen window sill.

When my mother's divorce from my father became final, she and Raymond and I traveled, on August 25th, 1956, to Carson City, Nevada, so they could get married. I was allowed to participate in their "wedding." Not a traditional wedding, of course, just three of us in a lonely little chapel behind the town's main saloon, where my new stepfather said "yeah" instead of "yes," and we hastily repaired to the saloon for gin and tonics. About a month following this strange ceremony, my mother and her new husband left San Francisco on a freighter bound for Europe, with plans for me to follow by air at the end of the summer with my grandmother. Just why she had decided to take us to Italy that year I'm not sure. I don't remember any conversations about this grand new adventure. Mom had this way of just making things happen when she set her mind to it.

What I loved most about North Beach was its foreignness; it felt similar to what I imagined living in a European country would be like: melodic language in the air everywhere, garlic and espresso, foreign newspapers left on the park benches, and the sour cigar smoke in the air. Living there made me feel I was different from most of the kids I knew, and I loved that. From very early on, I had wanted to be distinctive and unique, to stand out just like my crazy mother. And when I eventually arrived in Italy at the age of eleven and heard Italian spoken everywhere on the streets of Florence, it all felt familiar and safe, as though I had come home.

When I returned to North Beach decades later, most of the Italians were gone. My "village" was now populated by the Chinese who had come spilling out of a claustrophobic Chinatown to the south, with suitcases of money, and had bought out most of the Italian families, who then scurried off to the clean, flat, less complicated suburbs. No more cigar smoke and operatic dialogue in the park on Washington Square. Now it was morning Tai Chi exercises on the grass in front of St. Peter and Paul's, twangy Chinese music from boom boxes, signs in Chinese in front of the convenience stores, and lots of little children with chubby cheeks and perfectly bobbed haircuts. Gone were most of the dark coffee houses and Italian newspapers. And now there settled in the landscape a cautious dance between Chinese and white folks, as they eyed one another skeptically and maintained their distance. Happily, you could still get succulent focaccia at the Liguria Bakery on Filbert and Stockton, and most of the old time Italian trattorias remained.

Reflection: Life is uncertain, everything changes . . .

Stories from Two Houses in an Old Neighborhood: Pacific Heights

For as long as I can remember, Pacific Heights has endured as one of the truly rarified neighborhoods in San Francisco, spilling over some very steep hills to the north down toward San Francisco Bay, and stretching east and west along the very flat Pacific Avenue, where tall stone mansions with trimmed hedges and doors with brass numbers housed the well-to-do. It was quiet and clean here, the houses all had spacious garages, you rarely saw police cars here like you did in North Beach, and there was never a soul on the street at night. I inhabited two houses here, my grandmother's on Divisadero Street and my best friend Sue's home on Union

I probably spent more time growing up in my grandmother's home than in any of the places my mother chose. You see, she arranged it that way. She didn't know what to do with me most of the time, and my grandmother (my father's mother) had grown up motherless and all of her life wanted a daughter—happily took me on.

Grandmother's house at 3041 Divisadero Street was a subdued gray-and-white brick structure perched on a very steep hill at the base of Pacific Heights in the northern part of the city facing the Bay. Graceful tall windows with wrought iron balconies faced the street, and it stood tall and proud, four floors vertical, with a glossy black front door with beveled glass at the street level. Inside, a grand mahogany staircase led up to the first floor where much of our lives unfolded: dining room, kitchen, and a large gray living room with a fireplace at one end and quiet gold Japanese screens spanning the opposite wall.

My grandmother, who was Southern by birth, put a lot of stock in manners, and it was at her table that I received training in table manners, polite conversation, and accepting graciously what was offered. Her dining room had dark green walls and a curved set of windows that looked out toward the Golden Gate Bridge. An oil painting of an ancient Gadsden ancestor in an ornate gold frame hung over the antique English sideboard with its array of polished silver bowls and vessels. We always ate dinner here, my grandparents and I, and sometimes I was allowed to invite a good friend like Sue, who joined me in sitting properly at table and waiting with curiosity to see what steaming goodness would come from the kitchen. My grandmother's table was a picture of the Old World: an old lace tablecloth, engraved silver salt dish with dark red glass bowl and tiny spoon, four tall silver candlesticks, and the little straight crystal glasses from Venice with gold etching at each place setting. Grandmother sat at the head, facing the windows, and I always sat on her left, looking at the landscape painting of Charleston where she was born. This house was filled with history. Sue and I drank out of the little Venetian glasses; Grandmother had her wine, and we drank apple juice that we pretended was wine. She told us about growing up in the big house on Hassell Street in Charleston with a devoted nanny called Goldie, a stern but loving father, and no mother. She was a great storyteller, and her eyes sparkled as she described her old way of life, including the thoughtful conversations she'd had with her brilliant father, and as she spoke of this time, her accent subtly took on a lilting Southern rhythm.

We ate well here always. Daily, her tall African American housekeeper, was a humble but polished cook, serving us dinner usually in three courses: first a vichyssoise, then perhaps a golden brown roasted chicken with buttered rice and parsley, and perfect little French cut string beans. Some evenings, we were offered strange things like boiled beef tongue, one of my grandmother's favorites from the olden days, which we secretly thought was nasty but ate willingly because there was a sweet dark raisin sauce to pour over it. Daily always wore white, which made her dark skin look even blacker than it was, and she smiled widely, showing her brilliant white teeth as she moved from my grandmother to the others around the table. We grinned at each other a lot across the table as we gradually got used to being waited on. When Grandmother needed something from the kitchen, she pressed her small foot to the rug below where a buzzer was hidden, and we always got a kick out of that. The highlight of dinner was usually a perfect strawberry and chocolate ice cream and Daily's lace cookies that reeked of vanilla and crumbled to a wonderful sweet dust in our mouths. Before I snuffed out the candles with the long silver wand, we swished our fingers in the etched crystal finger bowls where a single brightly colored Venetian glass animal sat staring at us. While Grandmother sipped black coffee out of her tiny demitasse trimmed in gold, we munched on chocolate-covered mints.

Little did I know, as I lay in my twin bed in the guest room at night listening to my grandmother read softly from the Greek myths, that I would eventually become a student who was passionate about ancient literature and culture. The bedroom had dusty pink walls, two identical, four-poster twin beds, a pale maple dresser, and soft upholstered chairs by the bow windows. I could see from there the top of the brilliant orange Golden Gate Bridge, often draped in puffy white fog. As she read to me, turning the book to show me all the illustrations, she laughed about the egotism of the gods. "And it hasn't changed much over thousands of years, either," she'd add with a smile, hinting that large egos still got human beings into trouble. The bedsheets were always white, perfectly pressed and soft, and they smelled of lavender. I loved pulling them up around my neck and sinking into a little cocoon.

"Dearie, want to hear just one more?" she would ask, and of course I said yes. She loved this quiet time together, and when she bent over to kiss me goodnight, I could feel the cool dampness of her cheeks from tears that sometimes fell from her eyes—not from sadness but from a defective tear duct, I think. She had been ill with infantile paralysis as a young child, and it had permanently changed the shape of her face, elongating her cheeks and jaw and causing her mouth to slant downward. She had lived gracefully with this misshapen face since she was two, around the time she also lost her mother to TB. We both found motherly love during these evenings, something neither one of us had really had before. I was the daughter she never had, and she surrounded me with a mother's love always. She left the bathroom light on for me and the door ajar because I was frightened of the dark, and she reminded me I could come and get into her bed anytime during the night. My grandfather always slept in a separate bedroom, a little gray cell-like room next to mine, where he snored away as softly as the foghorns that moaned outside through the night.

Grandmother liked to take a bath in the morning before she dressed, and I often sat in the bathroom with her, watching her add bubble bath that smelled like old dry roses. I sat there and watched her slowly move her naked body that looked pretty old to me then, with its sagging pink breasts and sparse pale pubic hair. She paid little attention to her naked body, I guess because as a child she had been trained in modesty and circumspection. Once she had settled into the glittering bubbles in the tub, I'd ask her about when we were going to the symphony, or maybe nudge her to tell me about her life studying the piano in the twenties. I was curious about all the parts of her past she didn't talk about and suspected she had given up a lot to marry my chilly grandfather; as I got older, I wondered whether she felt she had missed out on the path of a serious pianist and a woman with *a life of her own*. As we continued our morning bathroom conversation, I played idly with the different flower-shaped soaps at the side of the sink and held her fluffy white towel for her while she luxuriated in the steaming hot bath water, her long face getting pinker by the moment.

Many decades later, she would—then eighty-nine and blind—take a fall in this same bathtub, into scalding hot water that would burn her across much of her frail body, and no one, not her granddaughter or her housekeeper, Angelina, would be there to prevent it. This fall came at what she knew was the final part of her life; she was approaching ninety and weary, had outlived most of her friends, and had been preparing in her private way to die for quite some time, feeling deeply the losses of old age. In the several weeks that followed the fall in the tub, she appeared to move seamlessly from suffering inside her torched skin as doctors bustled about suggesting pointless medical solutions, to letting go of therapeutic measures and receding peacefully and happily, and with her family's love and good wishes, into unconsciousness and quiet death.

The walls of her bedroom were a warm blue with a beautiful antique single bed along one wall. Old prints, a couple of family portraits, and lots and lots of books lived in this room. And a most beautiful baby grand piano: her shiny black Mason & Hamlin, which she had purchased in 1922 as a young bride when she'd moved to New York City. It lived over by the windows on the north side of the room. She and I often played Hayden and Mozart duets together with me leaning into her perfectly straight body. As I stared out the bedroom window at the cars plummeting down the steep hill, she told me about studying piano as a young girl in Charleston, and about how she was made to practice on a paper keyboard in order to preserve the sober quiet of her Southern home in the afternoons when everyone took naps. She moved north to New York at nineteen to further her musical studies, and never returned to the South to live.

Grandmother sounded wistful when she told this story, the way she had when she told me, many years later, the story of a hidden love—a surprising detour she took with an ardent beau whom she could never give herself to because he was already married, and because "passion is just too messy."

She proclaimed all this to me emphatically over her Chinese chicken salad on a spring afternoon in San Francisco when I was in my late thirties and trying to convince myself that romance was essential for a happy life.

I held her story close, not able to erase from my mind the image of a lone well-dressed gentleman standing at a railroad station waiting for his beloved to show up, a woman who would not, who could not come. It was straight out of Casablanca, with the stricken Bogart in Paris in the rain waiting with a heavy heart for Ingrid Bergman. Grandmother never shared this memory with anyone else in the family, and I think I understood why. It made her deeply sad to revisit this time and remember that she had settled for loneliness and lovelessness when she married my grandfather. There was never much visible affection between my grandparents, no touching certainly, just the presence of unflappable civility and good manners. She had bought her beautiful piano just before the birth of her first child, my father, and she played her way through early motherhood as a means of survival, I'm sure. There were as many stories living inside this piano, I knew this, as there were in the pale pine armoire from Italy on the other side of the room, which housed all her books in English, French, and Spanish, as well as her travel books, poetry, and her set of miniature Shakespeare volumes in soft red leather with gold lettering. There was a special scent inside this pine chest: musty old books and printing ink mixed with cedar.

My grandmother's kitchen was all white and sparkling with old-fashioned appliances, lots of tidy cupboards covered with pristine glass doors, and a black-and-white tile floor that shone with a soap-and-water cleanliness. She didn't spend much time in the kitchen, since her Charleston upbringing had trained her to be mistress of the house, not a cook.

Despite being raised in this rarified world, she treated her devoted housekeeper and cook with respect and warm affection; she consulted with Daily regularly over a late morning cup of coffee, making her own few suggestions for the dinner menu and for the special treats she wanted to have on hand for my Uncle Chris, like the hard salami and special crackers to go with his cocktails.

My father's little brother, Christopher, was a wild one, with straight hair shoved across his broad forehead, and a mouth that curled seductively when he smiled. He smoked and drank and chased women as though his life depended on it and confused my grandparents with his careless ways; he had, from the very beginning, captured my grandmother's heart. He was wild and uncontrollable like her brother Phillip, to whom she had been devoted; sadly, she seemed to be drawn to the reckless temperament that she feared so.

Our ritual before dinner was cocktails in the living room around her short mahogany Chinese table, with crackers, cheese, and salted nuts. In the early days, the drinks were made in the kitchen by my grandfather who measured the scotch and vodka most carefully; he was an investment banker by profession, and precision for him was all. One evening in the late seventies, after Grandfather had been gone for about ten years, we sat before dinner and visited with one another, as Grandmother kept a kindly, vigilant eye on her younger son. I was married then and on my own, but I stood in judgment of my uncle as he careened through his life, unemployed and manic, looking for a pretty woman or the next drink. It was so easy to stand in judgment when you kept your heart locked up around your own demons. I noticed how Chris took Grandmother for granted and that made me angry. I couldn't understand then that beneath his self-abandonment and restlessness was a deeply unhappy man who was driven to rebel against the harsh and distant father who was now long gone.

Grandmother asked me to go into the kitchen and check on the timing of dinner with Angelina, and so I went, thinking I'd take time to visit with her zany intense Russian housekeeper. As I peered into her pot of boiling beets, the kitchen door swung open and Chris burst into the room, making a quick turn toward the liquor cupboard. He grabbed the bottle of bourbon, held it up to his mouth and took a large swig. Angelina shrugged her shoulders, and I just watched. When he realized he had been seen, he slammed it down on the counter and said bitterly, "She has never approved of that second drink, you know . . . she gets that terrible disapproving tone in her voice when you're doing something she doesn't like. . . . Know what I mean?" Yes, I knew. My grandmother's life was about moderation, and he was excess incarnate.

Still, some sadness and then a little whisper of compassion stirred in me in that moment. My uncle, on whom I'd had a big crush as a child, whose shoulders I'd loved to ride on before being tucked into bed, was a ravaged man. I noted his bloodshot eyes, his once bright face now pasty gray, the un-pressed shirt.

"Chris," I said, looking to reach out to him, "how are things in your life these days?"

"Oh, great," said he too quickly, with forced cheer, "even though you never seem to call me anymore, Maggie. Remember those great old days . . . when you rode on my shoulders?"

I looked right at him, and said, "Yes," but it felt weird recalling old history. I was over thirty now, and those old times seemed to be disappearing from memory. I had discarded or lost track of the old childhood pictures.

"Now, get on out of here, you two," trumpeted Angelina, making shooing motions with her large arms. "I have a dinner to finish." I loved this kitchen of hers, all sparkly white and warm and smelling of roasted meat, but suddenly this cheery space felt sad and lonely. I looked my uncle in the eyes once more and walked through the swinging door back to the calm living room conversation, leaving my uncle's secret behind me. A few minutes later, he followed, returning to the gray living room looking miraculously upright and pulled together, and he was immediately blessed with one of his mother's smiles.

A decade later, in 1984, my husband and I walked up the grand staircase, and then the next, and into Grandmother's bedroom as she rested there with her morning tea, and we delivered the horrible news that her beloved son Christopher was dead, a sudden heart attack on a subway platform at age fifty-eight. And despite my fears that the news of her favorite son's early death would break her heart and kill her, my grandmother lived another four years with her characteristic courage and determination. She lived on because she was incapable of not persevering, of not inhabiting her own life.

The question of how we choose to live on interests me. Some people endure by forging ahead in their elder years, stripping away all the nonessentials and finding peace and acceptance as a monk might; some strive desperately to stay strong through yoga and tai chi and go off to trek in the Himalayas; and some go on expensive cruises to over-visited destinations like Puerto Vallarta or the Bahamas. Some simply sit in front of their television sets and wait for the inevitable.

The other San Francisco house that became my "home away from home" as a girl was the Landor house at 2516 Union Street in Pacific Heights, where my best friend, Susan, lived. It was an elegant shingled structure with a perfect view of San Francisco Bay through its panoramic living room windows, and a graceful pointed roof that poked out from over the redwood fence surrounding it. A sparkling glass front door opened into the entryway and the rest of the downstairs, and the dark-brown wooden floors always gleamed and smelled of fresh wax. I remember feeling when I came in the redwood gate from the street that I was entering a protected refuge: the deep red brick patio, pink fuchsias and red geraniums, and lush green foliage abundant in the front garden, and a few black canvas butterfly chairs where the patriarch of the family loved to sun himself.

While most of the action unfolded on the first floor of the house, there was a second living room above where their natural wood grand piano lived, along with the spacious black leather Eames chair and a sleek black-and white monkey hide rug. Abstract paintings in pale colors hung on the walls here, and despite the abundance of the art, there was always a Zen-like serenity in the space. Sue, her big sister, Lynn, and I inhabited the very top floor, which was painted stark white and felt like the secret attic in an old children's story. It was our hideaway, where the three of us could say and do almost anything. We stayed up late into the night in our attic, gossiping, telling secrets, and smoking Salems, and then later descending the two flights of stairs to Josephine's warm kitchen, with the black-and-white floor and grand black stove, to sit down around the table with a quart of coffee ice cream (a favorite when we were young) and some biscotti. We giggled a lot, and we talked about everything—the ice cream, school, our crushes, and our weird parents—held in this comforting bubble of home. We never doubted we were the best of friends. It wasn't until much later in my life that I was able to feel a gratitude, I didn't know how to express when young, for this comforting family.

There was a time when I walked through the redwood gate to 2516 Union Street and everything felt different to me. It was a golden San Francisco summer afternoon in 1973 and my best friend, Sue, was getting married. We hadn't seen each other for years. I had been traveling on a domestic treadmill of sorts with a husband and two little children, driving up and down suburban streets, trying to keep everyone's lives afloat, while she had been an urban single in the city, diligently pursuing a graphic design career in her father's successful company. Close as we had been when we were young, we now seemed to have drifted away from each other. I had been married about eight years by this time, long enough to have forgotten the promise and magic of love's beginnings.

The garden around the family's brown-shingled abode on Union Street was decorated with arbors and lights and flowers in abundance. Amid the fuchsias, roses, and ferns, over a hundred guests had gathered in the back garden for the ceremony, bubbling with conversation and exchanging kisses on the cheek; I entered the scene, feeling a little like an interloper. This day of celebration for my best friend gave me little joy, despite the big wow of Josephine's shimmering purple Thai silk, the beautiful chamber music, and the benign and proud look on her father Walter's face. My friend looked beautiful in the garden in her understated ivory gown and luscious black hair falling in a perfect wave down her back, and her new husband, Stafford, looked quite formal and buttoned up in a New England sort of way, trying his best not to be self-conscious. There were white and red roses everywhere, and people toasting with the best California champagne in etched crystal flutes. I couldn't quite get to Sue, I remember, to wrap her with a hug and offer her good wishes. I don't know whether it was my habitual choice of staying separate or my need to hold on to the melancholy I had become attached to. We were good friends too, sadness and I. Trying not to think too much, I downed my bubbly quickly. I was about to meet the man she had promised herself to for the first time, and I had the strangest feeling that I was being robbed of my best friend.

Everything appeared picture-perfect, I thought, as I bit into a chocolate-covered strawberry, and ghostly envy started to surface. Everything surrounding me was very tidy, very beautiful. Too perfect, I thought, as a fleeting memory of my own hastily arranged marriage in a little chapel on a college campus in Ohio surfaced in my mind. There had been no white roses or string quartets at our reception. On that bitter cold gray afternoon in January, I had worn a green wool A-line dress to camouflage my pregnant belly, and I remember looking to my new husband and the wedding day itself with more anxiety than hope. I had never been proposed to or given a sparkling diamond ring, nor was I able to show off in a flowing white gown. And as I looked upon all this grace in the Landor garden, I realized that I still held on to those fragile young-girl dreams of love and marriage, and this experience made me a little queasy. Early evening came, and we finally left the wedding party, walking out onto a quiet Union Street where sea breezes cooled us, and the sky was turning golden. I told my distracted husband that I felt I had been abandoned, but he had no clue what I was talking about. Of course.

When the Landor sisters sold 2516 Union Street decades later, following their mother's death in 2001, I felt that a part of me had been peeled away. But people move out, people move in, and we all move on. Because I was incurably nostalgic, I often made detours in my car to drive by the old house and take a peek, and for just a second bring to memory the kitchen, the garden, the camaraderie, and the beautiful mother. One such afternoon I discovered that the dignified old brown-shingled home on Union Street had been painted over by its new owners in a most surprising and unappealing pea green, which seemed an insult to its marvelous old-world character and its history.

Reflection: Love is the great healer.

The City's Center

City Hall's grand domed structure rises three hundred feet above the center of San Francisco and the district we call the Civic Center. This grand symbol of law and order has been a constant in my life in this city, which has endured a flood of changes: more and larger cars; more people, including the homeless population that has become an integral part of the landscape; the ripping away of antiquated structures in favor of the streamlined and modern; buses the length of half a block; and the forlorn presence of fast food venues such as McDonalds. I have always loved this grand building because it has history, real age. Completed in 1917 and dressed in the romantic architecture of the Beaux Arts, it is a San Francisco presence to be reckoned with. Right across Van Ness Avenue sits its sister building, the War Memorial Opera House. This pair of elegant Beaux Arts ladies house the city's government and its cultural traditions.

I have tripped by these two beautiful buildings throughout childhood, hopping on a Van Ness bus or marching into the opera house with my grandmother, and their endurance over time makes me feel at ease. City hall sports grand gold detail and Doric columns symmetrically positioned much like the really old stone buildings I've photographed in Paris or Rome, and it sits proudly in the midst of everything—the assassinations of our mayor Moscone and Supervisor Harvey Milk (if Supervisor is capitalized, shouldn't "mayor" be capitalized as well? It is a title, after all), the painful riots that followed, and the relentless and unceremonious attempts by law enforcement to "clean up" San Francisco by expelling the homeless and mentally ill from the park on the east side of the building. It has cast its shadow over political rallies in the square for everything from saving elephants to supporting immigration reform and celebrating Gay Pride. It was also a place of serious civic business. Back in 1991, I dressed myself up and marched in here to show up in court and petition my husband of twenty-five years for a divorce, an act of unfriendliness that took me decades to reconcile myself to. On that particular morning, I did not notice or love the grand marble in the hallways, the columns, and the ornate door fixtures, or the echoes of history—I was trying to clean up a mess so I could move on.

Starting from the time I was about seven or eight, my grandmother had outfitted me in proper dress to take me to the opera house, to hear both the symphony and the opera. My grandfather tagged along most of the time, and often snored his way through the final acts. I felt oddly at home there, because of the amount of time that I resided in another time in my imagination. Those late 1800s represented a velvety refined way of life that was, of course, bound to become irrelevant over time. And as I grew into adulthood, I saw all too clearly that we can no longer live in a cloistered world, nor should we. While its exterior is imposing, the opera house's interior feels intimate, its white marble foyer leading into the orchestra with plush red upholstered seats, cozy gilded boxes encircling the hall above, and a dazzling crystal-and-aluminum chandelier fanning out from the ceiling above. When I first came here, I told myself stories about the grand dark velvet curtains with gold fringe and kept my eyes on the two scary gilded masks at either side of center stage. The faces of comedy and tragedy seemed to be twins, each expressing something I couldn't understand. My head moved left and right as I looked into the large masks, to distract myself from sorting out the story unfolding onstage. I tried to figure out what was different about those faces . . . who exactly was sadness and who laughter? They anchored my attention, and today when I sink into my seat in the orchestra, I look up and think of them as familiar old friends. I sat through performances of *Madame Butterfly* and *Carmen* and *The Marriage of Figaro*, becoming filled up with the sprawling epic of opera: theater, music, dance, life, and death. My grandmother and I often talked on the way home about the stories, the costumes, the music, and the tragic endings. I don't remember ever feeling saddened by the tragedy, because I always felt safe in her company.

If I drive north up Van Ness Avenue today, past the Civic Center around Valentine's Day, I will see the grand rotunda of city hall lit up in brilliant red, the warmth of the color stretching outward into the night sky, reminding San Francisco citizens of tender feelings we hold as we motor forward in our daily lives. When the San Francisco Giants are in the playoffs, the grand building glows orange with the team's primary color; and on Election Day, we see the star-spangled red, white, and blue spreading into the sky over the Civic Center. The most joyful light show occurs during Gay Pride month, in June, when a wild rainbow of red, blue, pink, and yellow shouts out to the passing crowd that we are an inclusive city, a small world where people who have been outcasts find refuge, where they can march by the thousands down Market Street with bikes and banners and glitter, wildly painted faces and streamers, celebrating their difference. As with anything beautiful, however, this city has its underbelly. Greed is alive and well here, corporate and otherwise. Many old timers shake their heads at the glitzy modern structures going up everywhere when there doesn't seem to be enough cash on hand to feed the homeless, improve the educational system, or train our policemen. We have become a gentrified, in some ways much whiter landscape, many say, pushing out the middle class and attracting all the young "techies" who flock here to this beautiful place to make money. Will San Francisco lose its essential character because we are becoming a hub for the Googles and the Twitters and are being swallowed up by the voracious construction of expensive buildings? I would like to believe this isn't possible.

I have noticed that when people demonstrate and march in this city, it becomes a place where people smile at one another—on the bus, on the street, in the restaurants—and there is a more visible inclination to lend a helping hand. Love is generated in these isolated moments, as past injustices and cruelties temporarily fade—sort of the way things were in the late sixties when the hippies made San Francisco their home. What is it about the society and geography of this city that engenders this good will, this sense of expectation and possibility? I think it's a complicated coming together of right place/right time: this beautiful little hilly town with its international population, the streets spilling down toward the Pacific, its maverick colorful history still alive in the streets, parks, and stately Victorians, providing a landscape that invites creativity in art and music, political changes, good will and community.

Reflection: Culture shows us who we are, what we love

Landscape of Hills and Ocean

The fluid, rolling landscape of San Francisco has been my home. I've felt for a long time that I belong to the sea, and much of what moves me here is right at the water's edge.

On my eleventh birthday, my mother organized a party that took place at Playland at the Beach, an amusement park right across from the long straight expanse of Ocean Beach, where the city touches the ocean. She and a good friend supervised a small crew of us young girls as we wandered among the rides, the hot dog stands, and the cotton candy kiosks. It was a ratty and sad little park back then, with a drab carousel, small Ferris wheel, and a bumper car concession called Dodgem. The Fun House was a hodgepodge of weird, not-so-scary rooms filled with optical illusions and popup characters. The star of Playland was the roller coaster called the "the Big Dipper." As we came closer to it, I remember feeling that I just couldn't make myself do it—it was too scary. And then there was all that screaming. A few others in our group were wriggling about and laughing about whether they'd be brave enough to ride the roller coaster, and I just kept looking up at those little cars careening in the air and hearing the piercing cries. I hated heights, and the idea of a roller coaster made me sick to my stomach.

As everyone else got ready to line up for the ride, I held back, feeling queasy. It was my birthday, after all—could I really get out of this challenge? A friend of my mother's, a gay gentleman called Allan, set everything in motion when he said grandly, "Mag, darling, I'll give you this special silver dollar of mine if you'll screw up your courage and get on that ride today!" That was it. The bribe worked. I stuffed myself into a seat next to my best pal, and as we got going, I reached out for her hand. What happened next was a blur of heart-stopping terror as I kept trying to avoid seeing just where I was in space: up in the sky, it felt like, whirring sharply around to the left as I caught a glimpse of the gray ocean far below rippling over the beach, where tiny people moved about randomly. Sue screamed and shrieked like everyone else, although she didn't seem scared, but I was paralyzed. I could hear the groaning of the structure beneath the violence of our movements, and I put my head down as we dropped a frightening eighty feet on the tiny tracks. When we finally arrived back at the start, I was trembling, while everyone else swaggered about, proud of what they had done. I felt grateful for the solid ground underneath my feet as I snatched my silver dollar from Allan, and my stomach roiled at the greasy hot dog smell all around me. I don't remember whether I ever had a birthday cake that day, or exactly when I got my birthday presents, but I do remember swearing I'd never set foot on another roller coaster in my life. And about six months after this so-called celebration, Playland was torn down by the city, deemed too old and unsafe to maintain any longer.

Much later, as I was walking my dog Francesca along the same stretch of Ocean Beach, watching her golden fur become illuminated by the sun, I looked across the Pacific Highway to the place where Playland had once been, and I thought I could hear the screams and the clatter all over again and feel the wind whipping our faces high up in the air. This particular stretch of beach at the westernmost point of San Francisco is pretty unremarkable in most ways, straight and flat, separated from everything else by a large graffiti-covered concrete wall and stone steps. The seagulls always seem to be soaring overhead, and there is almost always a strong breeze from the ocean. I have never discovered any wonderful shells or sea glass or cool stones on this strip of sand, but I have always loved the feeling of my feet making prints in the dampness right next to the pounding ocean, watching those prints wash away, and feeling that piercing cold wind off the Pacific. This dog, who lived with me for more than fifteen years, always took this and all beaches in her stride, never getting loose like other dogs that seemed to morph into little race horses on the sand at the first whiff of ocean air. She didn't see herself as a dog. She was an old lady in a dog suit strolling with her best friend along the sandy beach. Like the surfers, the children, the loving couples, and the private souls who walked on this beach, she and I found solace here at the edge of the Pacific Ocean.

For those of us who have lived in the city for a while, the Embarcadero has always signified the old waterfront story of San Francisco and its rollicking gritty past. Many little "spider piers" reach out into the Bay all along the northern and eastern boundaries of the city where, during the early days, a sprawling and prosperous shipping business played out. During the heart of the city's economic boom, San Francisco was a center for shipping and commerce and ferry boat travel, and the site of labor strikes in the thirties, lots of seedy bars with funky neon signs, and some odd vintage buildings that housed artists who went to school on the GI bill in the forties and fifties. Shipping fell away eventually as two major bridges were built and a freeway was constructed along the length of it, immediately obliterating its graceful scale. The fishing and especially the shipping cultures began to wither. Soon it became a dormant landscape, with the exception of

Fisherman's Wharf at the northern end, a congested collection of large mediocre restaurants peddling seafood, steaming crab pots, and dozens of souvenir stores selling San Francisco trinkets made in China. Over time, the wharf became a destination for tourists from all over, as San Francisco became an international travel destination; the place seemed to have a life of its own, no matter how many locals derided its mediocre cuisine and honky-tonk atmosphere.

But the 1989 Loma Prieta earthquake that rocked the Bay Area spelled the beginning of a rebirth for the Embarcadero, as the freeway needed to be demolished, and then the street along the waterfront rebuilt and reinvented, with spiffed up streetcars from Italy, palm trees, and an imaginatively rejuvenated Ferry Building. When I stroll along this reborn thoroughfare today, watching ferry boats haul our visitors and commuters back and forth, and the little cyclos driven by cute muscular young men in shorts, my mind, which loves to hold present and past together at the same time, recalls the days when this place was gritty and lonely, and there were just a few little ratty streetcars running along by the water trailed by fat gray seagulls. From the time I was a child, I have loved the damp and smelly air here, that perfume of fish and salt water, reminding me of some of our little family's adventures by the water, like the night in 1955 when we set out to hear music at the Tin Angel right across from Pier 23.

My mother, stepfather, and I went more than once to this waterfront dive because Mom had worked there briefly as a cocktail waitress and because they had serious Dixieland jazz musicians. This night was special, because we were going to hear the great clarinetist George Lewis. This legendary jazzman was at the end of his long career, and he had brought his band all the way from New Orleans to show San

Franciscans something about Dixieland music. His records were just some of the many 78s that my mother had piled up chaotically in one corner of our dining room, along with Sidney Bechet and, of course, Louis Armstrong. Even though I was a kid, I was allowed into the club because they knew my mother and because the liquor laws in San Francisco at the time were pretty relaxed. It was a narrow, smoke-filled, claustrophobic space with a bar in the center, and small tables around the perimeter, and there were a lot of mirrors overhead so you could look up from almost anywhere and see the whole crowd below. I sat with my parents at a tiny circular table up close to the band, ate peanuts, and drank ginger ale, while everyone else sipped martinis in oversized cocktail glasses. I remember the clinking of ice, too, the glasses all sweaty on the tables, and the grumpy-looking bouncer dressed in black at the door, but I was really caught by the fragile old black man from New Orleans who looked as skinny as his shiny black horn. I stared through the gray smoke and tapped my feet to the beat as these black men in rumpled brown suits played their hearts out. I warmed to the sound of Lewis's reed, shrill and soulful at the same time, and when I went into sixth grade later that year, I chose to play clarinet in the band. My career as a clarinetist lasted barely a year, however, since I never figured out how to push enough air from my little lungs into the horn to make it sing.

Ships of all kinds sail into San Francisco Bay, and they all must pass under the Golden Gate Bridge, that strikingly orange span that is a central part of San Francisco's legend. Built in 1937, long before our family came West to California, it is the gateway to Northern California and the romantic lush landscape of Sonoma, Mendocino, and beyond. It is also the gateway to the vast Pacific Ocean from San Francisco Bay. I have walked across the bridge a few times in my life and each time felt as though I were suspended in space between an enclosed, known landscape (something safe) and the infinite sea (something deeply mysterious). This is the part of the bridge's character that's easy to love. But there is also its dark side. Stretching an impressive 220 feet above the Bay, this not so "golden" bridge has become over time the choice of thousands of men and women bent on ending their lives—hand eventually a series of unusual additions to the exterior were added to discourage suicide. I recently learned that approximately every two weeks someone tries to jump into the icy Pacific, and most of these stories of despair go unheard. I had an old friend named Bob Miller, a creative genius of sorts and a mentally tortured man, who jumped off the bridge to his death over ten years ago after an earlier failed attempt. I can't cross this bridge now without bringing him back into my mind.

Looking further back, I remember being on the Bay in a little vessel that was taking our family—my mother, my husband and daughters, and some friends—out to sea to scatter my stepfather's ashes in March of 1988. I looked up at the bridge when we cruised under it and wondered about that enormous distance through the air that a body would have to fall when someone jumped. There had to be easier ways to end one's life, I thought. I stood at the back of the boat along with some friends and my mother, looking back at the city's many hills rising, sparkling and pristine, in the sunlight, and realized I was going to have to help her pour the ashes into the water. My mother was nervous as she thought about letting go of Peter, her favorite among her three husbands; it was clear she wasn't ready to let go. In time, we did the deed. I will never forget the sandy gray ashes rising up in the air and blowing back, stinging our faces, as we looked at the city becoming ever smaller beyond the bridge. Most of the remains hit the water while the rest landed on us, which seemed fitting somehow. We opened another bottle of champagne to celebrate the occasion—Peter would have liked that—I noticed my mother wasn't crying, and finally we all cheered together as the Neptune Society's boat finally changed its course for home.

Reflection: The ocean is our home—a place of life and death.

Learning about Food

I generally felt more at home in restaurants as a child than in my own home. It all started when my mother began to navigate the life of a single divorcee when I was about eight. Much to my surprise, I was often included in dinners out with her and her artist friends—was she training me to be a grownup? All this meant many dinners out in San Francisco restaurants, from the rowdy family-style North Beach joints to starched white linen at hushed places like Ernie's on Montgomery Street. I quickly grew adept at placing myself at the table, napkin on my lap, and becoming invisible to the grownups around me as I studied menus and thought a lot about the food. Eventually, I was choosing such unlikely offerings as snails, raw oysters, cheese soufflés, and pâté de foie gras.

As the years passed, my tastes became pretty refined—I moved from steak and roast chicken to beef Wellington, coq au vin, and smoked salmon. Over the years, a clear pattern emerged in which I found myself lunching with my grandmother Dimond and dining with my mother and her friends, and when at home I began to experiment with cooking myself. Cooking for my family of two or three seemed the only way at the time to eat a meal before nine at night. I now see it as self-defense. I carefully copied the way my mother made pasta with garlic and butter or pesto sauce with lots of parmesan, and soon learned the tricks of a beautiful green salad, garlic bread, and sautéed zucchini. I worked away at these things over time, and eventually was able to produce an interesting array of food on the dining room table, after which I'd politely summon the cocktail-drinking crowd in to dine.

I thought about food a lot. I realized early on that good ingredients nourished some mysterious yearning inside. And though I occasionally hoarded and snacked on Three Musketeers bars and Oreo cookies, I lusted primarily for tangy sourdough French bread, garlic and butter, soft cheeses, avocadoes and artichokes, steaming egg pasta, and roast chicken with rosemary. I began to understand what real food was. I probably spent more time thinking about food than anything else, except maybe a good Nancy Drew mystery or my best friend, Sue. When I took a bite of perfectly cooked chicken or sucked on a soft green slice of avocado, it felt a bit like a warm hug. So, eating good food eventually became a theme in my young life, played out mainly in the hundreds of restaurants I entered as I grew up in an adult world.

San Francisco has always been considered a food lover's paradise. In the beginning, after the Gold Rush in '49, there were the old-fashioned fish houses that showed up, like Tadich's and Swann's Oyster Depot, which still serve their fresh no-nonsense cuisine today; then the Italian family-style eateries with long communal tables, steaming pasta al pesto, and generic bottles of wine; and hundreds of hole-in-the wall, plainly decorated Chinese places with dim lighting and the smell of greasy fried wontons. Then there were what they called the "continental" establishments, where waiters dressed in tuxedos, served up steak with béarnaise on good china, and poured wine into crystal from thick decanters that sat on the fine white table linens. These upscale San Francisco restaurants were born in the forties and thrived through the fifties and sixties—they were the smart places to go, to dine and to be seen; they defined the San Francisco dining experience for some time. My mother loved these places because they did such a polished job of offering all their customers the pleasing illusion of glamour. The tuxedoed waiters were terribly polite, and they always served a perfectly dry martini. These hushed rooms, where everyone was impeccably dressed, fed my romantic imagination as I thought of old forties movie sets where a dapper Cary Grant or a Bogie might walk in at any time. The dark-suited men (the waiters were always men in those days) seemed almost excessively attentive, and my mother lapped this up because it made her feel perfectly special. I have a suspicion it reminded her of her earlier New York life, her home, and her own mother.

Ernie's on Montgomery was one of these continental places that showed off rich maroon silk walls, burgundy carpets, and crystal chandeliers. The year was 1955. We sidled into leather banquettes, and the bowing and scraping began. "Madam, would you care for a cocktail?" (Always the first question).

"Oh yes! Martini very dry with extra olives, straight up." And she would then offer a perky upward gesture of her hand for emphasis. I usually went for ginger ale, or when I felt festive, a Shirley Temple with the sticky red grenadine and cherry.

We usually sat for a long time over cocktails, and I studied the menu looking for something new and different while the grownups around me talked of local politics or so-and-so's divorce. I usually ordered all three courses, starting with the raw oysters, all sparkling and wet with horseradish and red sauce, then maybe a steak with béarnaise sauce and some kind of overdone vegetable like steamed asparagus or green beans, and of course, ice cream or maybe a chocolate mousse for dessert. I ate and they talked. And the more they talked, the more I seemed to consume. My mother ate very little, pushing her food about on the plate just as her mother used to do, and smiling at her husband and guests; she slowly sipped her wine, she batted her eyelashes, and finally she pulled out a cigarette, which was immediately lit by a lurking waiter in his black penguin suit.

Lunch was a very different affair in my young life. I often went with my grandmother Dimond to her ladies' club downtown on Union Square, where we also shopped for clothes and people watched. The Town and Country Club was a small private club for women in a narrow brick building set in the midst of some shiny taller structures on the Square, and it was protected by a dark wrought iron gate and a soft-spoken Japanese doorman named Edward. "Good day, Mrs. Haas . . . How do you do, Mrs. Dimond?" he said with a slight bow. First it was up in the elevator to the third level living room where cocktails and little hors d'oeuvres were served. The living room was a gray-green, with plush green rugs and beautiful white-framed windows that opened onto the large square with its sea of shopping bags and sensible purses. Soft upholstered chairs, little dark wooden tables, and a grand fireplace at one end. Grandmother and I sat down, and she ordered her blonde aperitif, I ordered my ginger ale, and then the little brown rice crackers would arrive, left at our table by one of the women who scurried about in dark uniforms and starched white aprons.

I talked to her about school and the struggles I was having with the new Mozart minuet I was studying. After lunch we were off to buy a dress-up coat and some black patent leather shoes for my first opera outing in a couple of weeks. Sparkly Mary Janes were my favorites—they made me think of magic and of Dorothy's famous ruby slippers, and I couldn't wait to put my pudgy little feet in them. I felt elegant in these shoes, and my wobbly reflection in their mirror-like surface made me want to giggle. I noticed there were never any men at the club and asked her about that. "It is a club rule, dearie. This is a women's club, except our Saturday lunches when husbands are invited. Isn't that wonderful?" I got a kick out of this, I remember. Grandmother and most of these women around us who were her peers had married for status and convenience, and not necessarily for love, and they cherished time apart from their spouses.

"I married you for better or worse, but not for lunch!" a friend of hers had announced to her husband who was about to retire, and I could tell from the smile on Grandmother's face when she shared this anecdote that she concurred. Surrounded by these strong talkative older women in sensible suits and with lovely manicured hands, I felt at home.

When she had finished her little cocktail, we walked down a spiral staircase to the sunlit dining room, bustling with conversation and the smell of buttery vegetables and lemon tarts. Black-and-white tile floors, white linen on round tables, and pretty silver place settings. Grandmother often ordered a soft omelet with vegetables and a little saffron rice on the side. Uniformed waitresses served us the buttery green peas or creamed spinach, and perfectly round boiled potatoes with parsley from shiny silver bowls, along with platters of flaky brioche that also held tiny glass bowls with perfectly formed yellow butterballs. I think my favorite thing on the lunch menu was their chicken salad with lots of mayonnaise and celery and dark red grapes. At the end came the dainty little cookies on a silver tray: macaroons, meringues, lace cookies, and perfect tiny fruit tarts. A meal here always felt like a special occasion.

Grandmother usually had a demitasse of black coffee after dessert. Following lunch, we went back upstairs to the ladies' room to gather coats, reapply lipstick or "powder our nose," and say goodbye, passing by a dark green room on the right where little foursomes of women chirped happily to each other over cards. I had the feeling everyone knew and loved my grandmother here, and she returned their affection; this was her society, hers alone. She was always lovingly addressed as "Lavinia." I felt happy to be with her; I knew who I was then, and I was also named Lavinia.

You don't meet many Lavinias today, for it is a name steeped in nineteenth-century European culture. I did meet one recently in a San Francisco restaurant called the Zuni Café on gritty, bustling Market Street in the city. The charming bookish Lavinia waited on me one afternoon, and while we didn't develop much of a friendship, we were able to share a few things that we cared deeply about: food and books and writing. She was an earnest writer with perfectly curly dark hair framing her long face, and like so many struggling creative people her age, she had become a waitress in order to survive as an artist. Before the "farm to table" movement spread from California across the land and became cool and hip, a young woman named Judy Rodgers pioneered it here in this bright and spacious place, using her years of living and working in France to bring the freshest, most vivid and succulent dishes to the San Francisco dining public. She essentially recreated a lively French bistro that eventually everyone wanted to be a part of.

This multi-layered, geometrically composed space was once small and simple: a single triangular shaped room with white stucco walls, glorious tall windows that looked on the street, white paper on the tables, paintings on the walls, and an edgy menu of Southwestern fare. Before long, it grew both up and out to become a maze of white rooms where light streamed through and the tables still had that great thick white paper to doodle on as you settled into your experience. The white walls still show off adventurous modern art, and the waiters and waitresses are all clothed in classic European attire: white long-sleeved shirt, long black apron, black vest, and always a tie. A classy look.

A wood-burning oven lives at the center of the place, custom made in dark red brick and continually fed with thick brown logs; it burns away continuously and turns out what many feel is a legendary roast chicken, paper-thin quirky pizzas, succulent little quails, and whole fish. I think of the stove as the heart of the restaurant. Handsome young chefs are the guardians of the oven, and they move seamlessly in their sensible thick clogs and checkered pants, shoveling the pizza and affectionately pulling the chicken to be cut into perfect quarters. They work with Zen concentration in the midst of all the chaotic sound and movement. My favorite place to sit is a table where I can watch the action: the young cooks doing the same things over and over with beautiful precision, like the sharp precise whack of the chef's knife over the roasted bird, or the intimate gentle handling of the bread salad that will serve as its nest.

Each of the rooms where you dine is shaped differently, like a zany puzzle piece filled with sunlight that warms the customer and shows off the food on the table. When you come in from the street, you are greeted by a long copper bar that gleams and suggests a good time. The favorite pastime time of many people is to stand at this bar, sip a perfect limey margarita, and stare out at the unpredictable, unglamorous life unfolding on Market Street, a grimy landscape where homeless men and women march with carts and their ragged dogs, and where many of the storefronts are unkempt and forgotten. Zuni's spacious light-filled interior offers a transparency that allows you to feel a part of the untidy life moving along past the windows on the street.

What walks in the door is also remarkably eclectic: statuesque drag queens stunningly made up, European travelers in sensible shoes, poets and actors in interesting worn T-shirts, high society characters all done up in black and white on their way to the symphony or opera, and business people trying to manage the messy roast chicken alongside their laptops while conversing on their iPhones. I was there one October night for dinner and saw a parade of drag queens that took my breath away—tight-fitting, sparkling dresses in purple and scarlet slinking by, perfect makeup, and spike heels that carried their oversized bodies up and down the narrow white stairs with mysterious ease. They were on their way to the Exotic Erotic Ball, an annual celebration born in the Castro district, and they were certainly strutting their stuff, gold lamé bags and all. I had the sense I had never seen women quite that beautiful and female.

I have written letters and the beginnings of essays here while sipping a thick dark espresso and watching my neighbors navigate their maps of San Francisco. I have studied Madame Bovary during a break from college classes while slurping up icy raspberry granita with langue de chat (cat's tongue) cookies. I even fell in love with an artist over a bottle of Iron Horse champagne. And I have made some life-changing decisions while working my way through their greasy rich roast chicken and pencil-thin shoestrings with a dear friend. My favorite time here is late in the afternoon when the lunch crowd is gone, and the clean white expanse feels as though it's mine.

I was trained well as a young girl in the ritual of eating, and now am happy to sit for a long drawn out peaceful hour over a single Caesar salad and a glass of Provençal rosé. Late on Sunday is good too, around nine o'clock at night, upstairs, when I can get that little table for one tucked away in the corner and watch the animated visitors at the long tables close by, sharing their fritto misto and clinking their wine glasses in celebration. I know myself here. I am comfortable in my skin. I love watching people share their pasta, their meringue desserts, their pizza. I'm seeing food draw people together, nourishing, supporting, and giving joy. I always feel part of the landscape, no matter who has come to dine or how forlorn and lonely I felt when I walked in the door. Most of the time I eat alone, occasionally interrupting the solitude by asking a server about the rich chicken stock in tonight's soup, the unusual bitter greens I discovered on my plate, or more recently about the untimely death of Zuni's beloved chef and owner, Judy.

I thrive in this microcosm, surrounded by all variety of human eccentricities, where the dance of food and people and pleasure keeps presenting itself. In rarified moments like this, I realize that food itself is one of the few reliable links to the stories of my past. Under the very different wings of my mother and grandmother, I learned both the graceful rhythm of fine dining among tuxedoed waiters, and proper table manners at the old establishments like Ernie's and the Town and Country Club. And later in life, at Swann's Oyster Depot, the narrow claustrophobic seafood house run by descendants of the same family that started it in the late 1800s, I felt my love of San Francisco tradition come alive; and Sam Wo's, famous for its many tiny rooms, rude waiters, and greasy Chinese fare, reminded me of how comfortable I am with mysterious and uncharted places; and La Folie, the beautiful creation of a Michelin French chef with its apricot walls and artful food, gave me permission to consume food in its grandest operatic form and to become a gourmet without any apology; and Greens, perched on San Francisco Bay in a vast industrial space and serving up elegant vegetarian fare created by a Zen chef, marked a time in my life when I turned my attention to the healing ways of Buddhism and sought freedom from suffering; and Ideale, a North Beach haunt that returned me to Italy, my old home, and its great carbonara pasta crafted by a sweet young Roman called Maurizio, confirmed that my ultimate comfort (and teacher) has always been Italian culture; and Okoze, my neighborhood sushi joint where chefs boisterously shout "Hai!" at you when you enter and leave, serving up glistening fish that slides down your throat and cold sake in chubby little glass decanters, seems to attest to my love and gratitude for all things from the sea. In all these establishments and many more, I took my time at the table to settle into and understand the landscape of food, to learn about culture, and to feel taken care of.

Reflection: Food is art, it nourishes our hearts.

Being Here . . . Now

I find myself now in San Francisco in the year 2015, and I'm aware of the considerable time span that stretches back to when I slept in my grandmother's house in the fifties or trudged up the hill with Joe to go to Miss Love's class in North Beach. I walk this city now in a different way than before. Not only am I training my older body to become strong so I might be able to take on longer walks with my children and grandchildren in faraway places, but I am walking the hills of San Francisco and looking about with fresh eyes, almost as though I were a visitor, stopping to admire the golden light that showers itself over the old Victorians, or the tribes of young children in their prim school uniforms waiting for parents outside the white marble of Hamlin School, or the young couple in shorts walking their golden retriever (perhaps he is walking them?) down the precipitous Fillmore Street hill toward the Bay as they both talk on their cell phones. I gratefully inhale the salt water and smile as the cool fog rolls in through the Golden Gate and bathes my dry and thirsty old face. Sometimes it feels as though I'm seeing and sensing these things for the first time. . . . Yes and no.

This is my city, and my feet know the feel of the steep hills, my heart knows the special evening light that often reminds one of Italy or the damp fresh smells and the birdsong of early morning, before the cars and buses. I'm sure I could navigate my way to the Bay if I were blindfolded. When I am not plotting my next adventure to some unexplored place, I can pause and be happy that the soul of this city has changed little in fifty years. Yes, the streets are being torn up everywhere, high rises are on the increase, and south of Market, which used to be an alternative industrial district, has become thoroughly gentrified. The downtown skyline now looks more and more like Manhattan, this is true, but for me there is an invisible cultural continuum and authentic character here that reminds me of much older cities like Florence or Paris or even Rangoon. This is a city loaded with history and character.

Like many San Franciscans, I can love this place in the present moment with all its urban chaos, while at the same time remembering its elegant and raucous old story. And then there's the natural and lasting beauty of this place perched on its seven hills at the edge of the Pacific Ocean that con- jures maritime cities like Naples, Barcelona, or Venice, that all have a haunting otherworldly quality because they are connected to the sea. I have been drawn to the water all my life, and when I take a walk these days, I frequently end up at the water's edge, watching with curiosity as the mostly ignored seagulls fly overhead and scavenge for garbage, look- ing outward to the water at the many different vessels—some quaint little tipping sailboats, some big lumbering old gray freighters—and I'm reminded of the joy and the possibilities of boarding a ship to travel somewhere far away. I feel con- nected to the rest of the world as I stand to look out to sea.

San Francisco is dense with culture—the Irish, Rus- sians, Italians, Filipinos, Chinese, Japanese, and all the layers of Hispanics have found homes here and helped to define this unusual eclectic urban space. We have become a dense mosaic of cultures. When you get on a Muni bus these days, you often hear fragments of other languages spoken, and I love that. As I start to become invisible in the presence of the Spanish or Chinese or Russian voices, I feel a sense of unexpected possibility. I have been lost that way in Venice, in Mexico City, and in Hanoi . . . and now I find I can get lost that way in my own city. Being lost seems to be an essential part of traveling—it leads to great new discoveries.

But what I love most is standing at the water's edge after my walk and allowing my imagination to dance in the salt air. While this hungry mind of mine inhabits an old body, it seems to grow younger and more vibrant every year. My grandmother's drive to learn all she could about the unknown, my mother's quirky ill-fated romance with art, an old friend's lifelong loyalty, my young family's constancy and love, even my father's essential loneliness—they all fill me up, remind me that love is possible here and now. All these beings propel me forward to understand and devour more of experience, to celebrate it the way I would a perfect oyster, a piece of dark chocolate, a great read like Anna Karenina, a Bach Invention, any painting by Matisse, or even an exquisite moment of mindfulness and the Buddha's love.

Acknowledgments

D eep gratitude to Sean Murphy and Tania Casselle, my stalwart and wise writing coaches, without whom this book might never have been written.

Bows to Jack Kornfield, my spiritual guide and dear friend, who always reminded me that I was an artist and thus had gifts to offer this world.

Without my grown daughters, Tara and Sara, who have taught me so much about family, I could not have reached the deep insights needed to explore my own very complex familial landscape. They are jewels in my life's mosaic.

About the Author

Mag Dimond has been a world traveler since her mother took her to live in Italy from ages eleven to fourteen. She traveled extensively in Europe and Central America, and ventured to such exotic landscapes as India, Cambodia, Bhutan, Japan, Kenya, China, Burma, Vietnam, Thailand, and Cuba. After a career teaching writing to college students in San Francisco and Taos, she now volunteers as a writing tutor at 826 Valencia, an esteemed literacy program launched by David Eggers. She is a practicing Buddhist and dedicated member of Spirit Rock Meditation Center north of San Francisco. Excerpts from Bowing to Elephants have been honored in American Literary Review, Travelers Tales Solas Awards, the Tulip Tree "Stories that Must be Told" awards,

and the 2017 William Faulkner Wisdom Awards. Addition-
ally, Dimond has published essays at Elephant Journal, an
online magazine with a readership of almost two million. You
can find her essays on her website, www.magdimond.com.

Author photo © Susan Landor Keegin

SELECTED TITLES FROM SHE WRITES PRESS

She Writes Press is an independent publishing company founded to serve women writers everywhere. Visit us at www.shewritespress.com.

The Coconut Latitudes: Secrets, Storms, and Survival in the Caribbean by Rita Gardner. $16.95, 978-1-63152-901-6. A haunting, lyrical memoir about a dysfunctional family's experiences in a reality far from the envisioned Eden—and the terrible cost of keeping secrets.

Godmother: An Unexpected Journey, Perfect Timing, and Small Miracles by Odile Atthalin. $16.95, 978-1-63152-172-0. After thirty years of traveling the world, Odile Atthalin—a French intellectual from a well-to-do family in Paris—ends up in Berkeley, CA, where synchronicities abound and ultimately give her everything she has been looking for, including the gift of becoming a godmother.

Learning to Eat Along the Way by Margaret Bendet. $16.95, 978-1-63152-997-9. After interviewing an Indian holy man, newspaper reporter Margaret Bendet follows him in pursuit of enlightenment and ends up facing demons that were inside her all along.

Motherlines: Letters of Love, Longing, and Liberation by Patricia Reis. $16.95, 978-1-63152-121-8. In her midlife search for meaning, and longing for maternal connection, Patricia Reis encounters uncommon women who inspire her journey and discovers an unlikely confidante in her aunt, a free-spirited Franciscan nun.

A Leg to Stand On: An Amputee's Walk into Motherhood by Colleen Haggerty. $16.95, 978-1-63152-923-8. Haggerty's candid story of how she overcame the pain of losing a leg at seventeen—and of terminating two pregnancies as a young woman—and went on to become a mother, despite her fears.

Home Free: Adventures of a Child of the Sixties by Rifka Kreiter. $16.95, 978-1631521768. A memoir of a young woman's passionate quest for liberation—one that leads her out of the darkness of a fraught childhood and through Manhattan nightclubs, broken love affairs, and virtually all the political and spiritual movements of the sixties

PeCone
Laura Predd
1500 Kudi Road
Apt 225
Zip 11944

CPSIA information can be obtained
at www.ICGtesting.com
Printed in the USA
FSHW011051030519
57813FS